BLACK SHEEP

MY JOURNEY FROM EVANGELICAL CHRISTIANITY TO ATHEISM

CASSIE FOX

This book is dedicated to every person who has demonstrated the bravery and courage necessary to live his/her own authentic truth.

THE FIRST DOUBT

I sat in fourth grade, observing the students in my classroom. It was the mid 1980s in a small, midwestern city of about 60,000 people. AIDS paranoia was on the rise, perceived as the punishment of God onto gay people. Ronald Reagan was the president of the United States and God's chosen one.

The first Macintosh computer had recently been introduced. We would all soon watch in horror as the Challenger space shuttle exploded right before our eyes. The first hole in the ozone had been reported.

I had other things on my mind, however. It was my first day attending public school, and I had no idea what to expect.

Until then, I had attended a small, evangelical Christian school. I had been living in an exceptionally tiny bubble, and God was intricately infused into every single component of that bubble. It was all I had known. Teachings about God and obedience had been woven into every subject of study and every aspect of my life.

God had been in my grammar lessons. He had been in my

math books. Science lessons were entirely about God's creation and how he designed the world. No alternative views were offered or even mentioned. Doubts and questions were never welcomed.

All of my fellow students had been from evangelical Christian homes like mine. That was my world. It was all with which I was familiar.

But, financial changes within my family had resulted in my parents' inability to pay for private education any longer. So, I found myself in public school for the very first time, and I felt as though I had been placed on a different planet.

I was incredibly intimidated by my new, fellow students. They were not Christians. They were different from me. They were on the side of the devil. Or so I'd been told. I did not know how to talk to these children. Thus, I didn't.

I sat quietly at my desk and watched the activity around me. I could only blindly guess what the school year ahead of me would hold. Amongst my list of guesses, however, I had not included the possibility that it would be filled with teasing and bullying. But, that is what happened.

That tiny bubble in which I had lived had left me ill-prepared for the outside world, and it showed through my social awkwardness. The children in my classroom picked up on it immediately, and the ridicule that resulted was relentless. School quickly became a terrible place of dread.

At church, I learned why. The students in my class were without God. All of us were born evil, and only by accepting God could we become good. No wonder the kids at school were so mean.

After all, look at how the heathens had treated Noah. But, they got theirs in the end. God sent a flood that covered the entire earth, and they drowned. I imagined how the Israelites felt as they endured their slavery in Egypt under the wicked hands of the pharaoh. The Egyptian army drowned in the end, too.

The world was vile, and I had to persevere through its darkness. This world was a place of suffering and misery. Someday, we would leave this fallen, temporary residence and enter heaven where we would live forever in joy and happiness. That was the real goal.

Still, deep down, I wished it were different. I wanted the children to like me. I wanted to be accepted. I wanted them to play with me on the playground and pick me to be on their team in gym class. But, it would never happen.

My desires for acceptance brought tremendous guilt. I was not supposed to want to be liked by these kids. They were worldly and godless. I was to be different. It was wrong to want to be the same.

Since the children would not be my friends, I spent a lot of time alone. I occupied myself at home quite well and often played by myself. I had a record player and spent long periods listening to it play music. I had a microscope and chemistry set. I loved making microscope slides and meticulously conducting little science experiments.

I often purchased old radios and other electronics from neighborhood garage sales and took them apart in efforts to figure out how they worked. I was incredibly curious about the world around me.

I was not particularly feminine. I paid little attention to dolls, though I had a collection of stuffed animals that I deeply cherished. I still have a few of them to this day.

I loved animals and learning about them. I was fascinated by the unique qualities of the many different species throughout the earth. I enjoyed occasional television programs about animals living in different parts of the world.

In the late 70s, the local grocery stores had become highly

competitive. They began offering special, limited sets of bakeware, books, and other items. One piece of the collection would be released weekly to encourage consumers to choose their store.

One of these local stores offered a set of 28 animal encyclopedias, releasing one book each week. My mother received every book in the collection except one. Throughout my childhood, I spent hours upon hours looking through this set of books, mesmerized by the different species living throughout the earth.

One of my most beloved activities during my earlier years happened whenever my dad would set up a rather large telescope in the back yard. He and I would sit outside and use it to look into the night sky. I had a chart of the constellations, and we would look for them when the sky was clear. Those memories are invaluable to me.

All in all, it would be fair to say that I was a nerd.

CHURCH

I attended church regularly. For a child so convinced that Jesus was the way, the truth, and the life, I did not enjoy going to church very much. I hated wearing dresses, which was required of me every Sunday morning.

Sunday mornings, I first attended Sunday School for one hour. Then, all of the children joined together in a large room for children's church. We began by singing children's songs about the stories of the Bible. Such songs were often sung while we all performed physical motions that accompanied the lyrics.

We marched and motioned as we sang,

I'm too young to march in the infantry
Ride in the cavalry

Shoot the artillery
I may never fly o'er the enemies
But, I'm in the Lord's army

I'm in the Lord's army
Yes, sir!
I'm in the Lord's army
Yes, sir!

We pretended to cast fishing rods into the sea as we sang,

I will make you fishers of men,
Fishers of men, fishers of men
I will make you fishers of men
If you follow me

If you follow me, if you follow me
I will make you fishers of men if you follow me

In a room filled with only white children, we stood and sang,

Jesus loves the little children
All the children of the world
Red and yellow, black and white
They are precious in his sight
Jesus loves the little children of the world

We held out our hands together as though they were a book, and we proudly sang,

The B-I-B-L-E
Yes, that's the book for me
I stand alone on the word of God

The B-I-B-L-E

When the songs were over, we were instructed to sit in our chairs and listen to the lessons until church was over. This typically lasted well over an hour, and I loathed children's church because of it.

Sunday after Sunday, I sat quietly and obediently in my chair, longing for it to be over. Every minute drug on, feeling as though it had no end. On weekdays, I dreaded school, and on weekends, I dreaded church.

My family did not often attend church on Sunday evenings. When we did, it was a rather confusing experience when I was a child. There were no activities for children during the Sunday evening services, so we had to stay with our parents in the adult service.

Just as in children's church, we began by singing songs. But, rather than specific motions, the adults would often seemingly randomly raise their hands into the air as they sang, a sign of worship to God.

Sometimes, someone would stand up and shout strange sounds. Everyone would immediately grow silent. As a young child, this always shocked and perplexed me. No one explained what was going on or why the person was doing this. I'd peek over the pew as I tried to see who it was that was making these strange noises.

Whenever the person finished, someone else would then begin shouting, but this time, it would be actual words. Through this entire production, everyone sat or stood in reverence and utter silence. I had no idea why.

Yes, my church was Pentecostal. We spoke in tongues, danced, got slain in the spirit, cast out demons, prayed for miracles, and shouted. The strange sounds I heard were coming from a person who was supposedly sharing a message directly from God for the people to hear in the language spoken in heaven.

This was then followed by an interpretation in our own earthly language. God would speak to someone in the congregation who would share the translation of what was spoken. This practice is still happening today in Pentecostal churches all over the world.

As a child, the chaotic environment of people rolling around on the floors, dancing, shouting, and more was frightening to me. I was glad we did not often attend Sunday evenings.

On Wednesdays, I attended Missionettes, which was the Christian version of Girl Scouts, though a lot less fun. While we girls sat in Missionettes and learned how to cook, clean, and quote Bible verses, the boys attended Royal Rangers where they made canoes, shot bows and arrows, sat around campfires, and more.

I longed to be in Royal Rangers. I could sometimes see them outside on their adventures while I sat inside and learned how to be a godly woman who cared for her household properly. Once, I had been misbehaving in class, often talking and interrupting. My Missionettes leader walked me down the hall to speak with the elderly woman who oversaw the program.

"This girl needs a lesson about how to sit like a young lady in a chair," my leader explained in exasperation.

The program director calmly replied, "Well, that is why girls should wear dresses."

THE FIRST SEED OF DOUBT

The fourth grade in the public school continued on to its completion. I struggled greatly with the rejection of my peers, but persevered. What other option did I have?

Fifth grade began, and that year brought about the first wave of information that caused me to question what I had been taught, even if only ever so slightly. Until then, America had been presented to me as God's country.

America was a nation that had been founded by Christian men who had turned away from the evils of the world. Our country was intended to be a land where all could worship God freely...but, only the Christian God, of course.

Our country, since then, had been corrupted, and it had turned from God, moving away from its original purpose. It was our duty to be good soldiers of Christ to take back our country for God. Nationalism was a core component of our faith.

I had envisioned our founding fathers attending church, singing to and praising God, and living the holy lives we were all called to live. This was what I had been taught, and I believed it fully.

My fifth grade history class then revealed a stain upon our history that had previously been hidden from me: slavery. In horror, I learned how men and women were abducted from Africa, chained onto ships, taken to our country against their will, and shoved onto platforms where they were auctioned off to slave owners and branded like cattle.

How could this be? George Washington approved of this? He was a part of it? How could someone be a Christian and do these terrible deeds? I did not see how that was possible.

I went home and shared with my dad that I did not believe our founding fathers were Christians. My dad became enraged and questioned why I would say something so shameful. I described what I had learned about slavery and explained that I did not believe that they could do such things and be Christians.

My dad refused to continue the conversation with me at that time.

MY PARENTS

Religion had been prized by my father since shortly after I was born, and he became livid when someone doubted his chosen faith. Religion had provided a haven for him that he had been unable to find anywhere else. Thus, he defended it with extreme intensity.

My dad suffered from anxiety and depression his entire adult life. His anxiety would become so severe, his hands would shake. Sometimes, he would even vomit. Before finding God, he turned to booze to alleviate these symptoms.

In my dad's defense, there were not a lot of helpful options to manage severe anxiety and depression back then. Evangelical Christianity, particularly television evangelists, provided my dad with something he needed to cope. To him, it was a perfect substitution for alcohol.

The mixture of music and smooth words used in many pentecostal churches can have a very powerful effect on the mind and emotions. For my dad, this became like a drug he used to self-medicate. He bowed in the living room one night as a preacher on television led the sinner's prayer, and he dedicated his life to God.

He never touched alcohol again. To him, living for God meant living to watch Christian television and send them his money. Throughout my childhood, my dad spent more and more time watching television evangelists until eventually, by the time I reached late childhood, he had lost all of his friendships and stopped all activities and outside interests in favor of these programs.

He stopped going to the tennis and basketball courts to compete with his buddies. The telescope sat in its box in the basement, collecting dust. I would never sit in the back yard and watch the stars with my dad again.

During the 80s and 90s, more effective medications and

treatments for anxiety and depression became available. However, by then, my dad had read a book written by Jimmy Swaggart claiming that the field of psychology was inspired by the devil. Mental health issues were demonic and required prayer, not medical treatment.

My dad accepted this completely and refused all treatment for his mental health after that. My dad continued to endure terrible anxiety and depression and to turn to television evangelists to cope until the day of his death.

My mother faithfully stood by his side through it all. She carried plenty of emotional issues of her own. Her parents had married and divorced twice when she was a child. Her father was an alcoholic, and his addiction affected her greatly. Her mother remarried, and her step-father was borderline abusive toward her. My mother had never healed from these wounds.

My parents needed therapy. Instead, they received religion. My mom witnessed my dad completely give up alcohol immediately after finding God. After her experiences with her own father, who had never succeeded in overcoming his addiction to alcohol, she accepted the Christian God as the answer to everyone's problems.

Together, they then based our family and my upbringing on evangelical Christianity. It was not to be doubted. It was not to be questioned.

Now, their 5th grade daughter was coming home from public school and claiming that the founding fathers of America might not have been so Christian after all. That evening, I was shamed for suggesting that someone like George Washington was not a Christian simply because he owned slaves.

The enslavement of black people was just how things were done back then, they explained. It was not a big deal. How could I even think such a thing about our founding fathers? My line of questioning was not going to be tolerated.

I did not understand this. God was the same yesterday, today, and forever. If slavery was wrong today, how could it have been acceptable back then? I wondered if the people who had been enslaved would agree that it was no big deal.

However, tremendous guilt and shame had been thrust onto me for speaking up. I was humiliated and mocked by my family. I felt filthy for having asked these questions. My desire to continue to wonder was squelched.

It was my first seed of doubt. I buried it deep into the ground of my mind. It would take many, many years, but eventually, this seed would sprout and grow.

DEEPENING FAITH

E lementary school was finally over. I had endured tremendous bullying, teasing, and ridicule from my peers. I could not have been happier to walk out of that school, knowing I would never return.

Sadly, one cannot walk away from three years of such treatment unscathed, especially during childhood. By then, I felt that I was ugly and stupid. My fellow students had been sure to make me feel this way.

I was often sad and lonely. I was in pain, and no relief could be found. I wished that I were someone else. I thought of the popular kids in my class and simultaneously hated them and desired to be them.

CHURCH CAMP

My mother informed me that she and my dad had registered me to attend a week-long camp with our church that summer. I was excited, considering it would be nice to get away from everything.

I anticipated long, peaceful walks in the woods, silly, fun

arts and crafts, and lots of swimming in the lake. This camp, however, included much more. The evening church services, which were held every day, were intense. I had never experienced anything like it.

The music was loud, and the kids and teenagers around me sang and worshipped with a level of passion I had never before witnessed. The preachers were eloquent and inspiring.

The environment this created was potent. It elicited extremely powerful emotions. I felt tremendous joy and excitement. It were as though a force rushed through my veins, delivering burst after burst of elation.

We were told that what we were feeling was the presence of God. To a group of suggestible young people with very little experience in the real world, the explanation was compelling.

For me, God, up to that point, had always been a character living far away, high in the sky. He watched us all of the time, and it was therefore very important to obey his every command. I had never considered the idea of God coming down and being with me right there.

They said God was indeed right there with me, and all of these extraordinary emotions were caused by him being present with me, loving me, and touching my heart. It was overwhelming, all-encompassing, and exhilarating. I had just endured three terrible years of constant rejection and cruelty from my peers. This entire experience spoke to my wounded heart.

It was firmly pressed upon us that we were the final generation before Jesus returned and God had chosen us to spread the Gospel in these final days. Our generation was extremely special and like no other.

I felt so honored and privileged. These were the most important days that had ever occurred in the history of the world, and I was chosen to be an important component of those days. There was a specific, eternally important reason for my life. For the first time, I felt that I really mattered in the world.

This message, combined with the intense atmosphere, changed how I approached my religion. While this world was dark and painful, I was not simply a feeble person trying to get through until I reached heaven.

I was a light in the darkness. I was a warrior for the army of God. I had purpose and meaning. It was my job to show these wicked peers the love of Jesus so they, too, could experience what I had experienced.

It was the love, purpose, and acceptance I had longed for. I returned from that week at camp with a completely different perspective about my life and the world. That one week was so profound for me, it would impact the next 15 years of my life.

SCHOOL AND SCIENCE

I entered the seventh grade the following fall with a new sense of purpose. I joined the youth group at my church, and we were a very closely knit group. There, I met the person who would be my best friend throughout high school. We did everything together.

I had found the love and acceptance I had previously lacked. It was a drastic improvement from my years at the public elementary school. On top of that, church had gone from being a place I dreaded to being a place I wanted to be as much as possible. I loved being there.

It was not all rainbows and roses, though. As I got older, my love for science began to be questioned and frowned upon. I was informed that scientists were atheists with a primary mission to destroy God. They were liars, and they faked data to deceive people into becoming atheists. Science, therefore, was a devious field of study, and no true Christian would desire such a thing.

The elective science courses I had taken thus far were the most enjoyable component of my entire educational experiences. I loved sitting around the lab tables conducting experiments with my peers. My teachers often complimented me as I was quite adept at learning the information. In my science courses, I had felt good about myself.

Now, I felt overwhelmingly guilty. There was this part of myself that I loved so much and that brought me so much joy, but it was evil and wicked. It was against God. I felt ashamed that such desires were even within my heart.

The treatment I received regarding my love for science was humiliating to me. I felt that I was letting everyone down. Most significantly to me, I was letting God down.

I stopped enrolling in science classes for my elective courses. After that, I lost interest in school entirely. I stopped doing my homework. I never studied. I did not pay attention during any of my classes.

What was the point in learning all of this? Jesus was returning very soon. The rapture was drawing nigh when God would lift all of the Christians into heaven, leaving everyone else behind to suffer through the great tribulation. What reason was there to spend time on such worldly things when we were living in the last days?

In retrospect, I understand that when the one subject of study that brought me joy and wonder was taken from me, I lost interest in education altogether. I had been made to feel so ashamed for simply wanting to learn about the world that I stepped away from it all.

Everything in my life was about my faith. I attended church every time the doors were open. I studied the Bible and prayed daily. I played multiple musical instruments, and

I had been taught that when I played, it must be done as worship unto God. So, I played for God.

Evangelical Christianity provides a cookie cutter one must fit into. I worked fervently to fit into that mold. Over time, I lost all sense of personal identity. My identity was to be in Christ and nothing else. That is what I strived for. There was no me anymore. There was only Jesus.

In spite of all of my extreme efforts, though, throughout this time, there was a yearning deep in my heart that could not be answered. I did not understand what it was. I was pursuing God with all of my heart. Still, it lingered. Many years would pass before I understood its cause.

CHURCH

In the youth group I attended, there was tremendous pressure to reach three milestones. The first was to receive salvation. I had already done so.

The second milestone was to be baptized in or filled with the Holy Spirit as evidenced by speaking in tongues. We were taught that when people become baptized in the Holy Spirit, the power of God fills them completely.

When people are baptized in the Holy Spirit, the joy of the Lord shines through them much more brightly. The lost are attracted to these people all the more because God can clearly be seen in them. The first sign that a person has been filled with the Holy Spirit is the person begins to speak in tongues.

I watched many young people walk to the altar during youth group services and ask God to fill them with the Holy Spirit, and I watched them begin to speak in the so called heavenly language. I desperately wanted this for myself so I could be a better Christian and live a life that is more pleasing to God.

I prayed again and again over the course of a year, asking to be filled with the Holy Spirit. I begged God. I was certain that that would fill this longing in my heart. That must be the missing piece.

At church camp the following summer, I stood at the altar as a group of teenagers gathered around me. We prayed together that I would be filled with the Holy Spirit. The minister came up to me and placed his hands on my shoulders and began to shout in my face, commanding me to be baptized in the Holy Spirit.

He continued to shout and command me to speak in tongues. The music was playing loudly. The teenagers crowded around me were crying out to God on my behalf. I almost felt as though I were in a trance. This surely had to be the moment that it would happen for me.

I did not know what else to do but to begin speaking something. Everyone was waiting for me to do something. I opened my mouth and began to utter sounds that were pure gibberish. Once I started, it was amazing how easily these sounds flowed from my lips. I realized I was speaking in tongues.

The minister and the teenagers began to shout in celebration. It had finally happened, I believed. God had filled me with the Holy Spirit. He had heard my prayers and seen the desire of my heart.

I was elated. I praised God and thanked him for answering my prayers. I cried in joy and gratefulness.

My faith deepened all the more. It was an affirmation. I took this to mean that if I just took a step of faith, God would take care of the rest. I soon discovered, though, much to my disappointment, that the longing in my heart remained in spite of it. Something felt amiss. I could not put my finger on it, but it was always there.

The third milestone in my youth group was to be called

into the ministry. Now, it is not that we were told everyone must be called into the ministry. However, there was extraordinary pressure to do so.

Frequently, one of the members of our youth group would announce he or she had been called into the ministry, and everyone would clap, cheer, and praise God. Those members of youth group were then treated as though they were elevated above the rest.

Our youth pastor spent more time with them. They were treated with greater respect. They were the most popular kids in the group. No one ever applauded or cheered when a member of the youth group shared that he or she had decided to be a physical therapist or a school teacher.

It is not surprising that, in that atmosphere, I, too, began to feel I was called into the ministry. I prayed and sought God earnestly for long periods asking if this was truly his plan for my life.

One night, during youth service, I believed with all of my heart that God had spoken to me and revealed with certainty that I was indeed called into the ministry. I knelt in my seat there in the sanctuary and accepted his call.

I had previously planned to be a music teacher. But, God's call was a greater purpose according to my understanding. I placed those plans onto the altar and left them behind. I determined I would never look back.

I was not searching for applause or accolades. In fact, I did not even announce my call to the ministry to my youth group like many others had. Still, in retrospect, I can see how that church environment impacted me during this vulnerable and impressionable time of my life.

I was going to be graduating from high school soon, so there was little left to do, in my mind, but prepare to attend Bible college where I would be trained to be a minister. My grades had been very poor in school all this time as I barely passed my classes.

Now, I had a reason to study and do well. I needed to learn how to take notes, write papers, and prepare for exams. Otherwise, how would I pass my classes in Bible college?

My senior year of high school, I buckled down. I paid attention in class, completed my assignments, and prepared for the exams. My grades that year were excellent. Meanwhile, my time at church intensified all the more as I excitedly awaited ministry.

THE SECOND DOUBT

During this year, I began to notice something rather peculiar. Speaking in tongues was a regular part of church services, both youth and adult. I began to notice that the syllables and "words" each person used when speaking in tongues were very repetitive and unique to each individual.

For example, one individual in our youth group often rolled his tongue every third word or so when he spoke in tongues. He also seemed to say the same syllables again and again, such as RA-MA-SHA-KI-NA with only slight variations in their order.

Another individual in our youth group used a different set of syllables, such as ME-KO-MUM-BI-HA-NA, but still a very limited set. She also was very repetitive with only minor changes in the order of these supposed words.

Everyone seemed to have their own small set of syllables that they said again and again virtually every single time I heard them speak in tongues. If they were speaking in a heavenly language, why did everyone sound so different from one another? Part of this aspect of my faith seemed made up.

Remember that in Pentecostal services, it is common for

an individual to feel that God has a message to share with the congregation through him/her. This person will begin to speak in tongues very loudly, sharing the message in the language of heaven, and all will immediately grow silent to listen.

Once the person has stopped speaking in tongues, everyone waits until someone else feels that God has granted him/her the interpretation of the message. That individual will then begin to shout a translation in English. I sat through countless episodes of this during my years attending church.

In spite of the small number of syllables spoken by each individual I heard speak in tongues, when they spoke loudly for all to hear in a service and an interpretation followed, the interpreted message was always much more complex than the original message given in tongues. The message in tongues would seem to be the same words spoken again and again, but the interpretation was never the same words spoken again and again.

The lengths often seemed to conflict as well. A message in tongues would sometimes be very long while the interpretation was very short or vice versa. It did not make sense to me.

However, it is difficult to pursue such questioning very deeply when one is locked into a mindset that defines her entire identity. To accept speaking in tongues was not real would mean I would have to question everything I had been taught. That is a terrifying proposition for someone who's entire being is founded upon such teachings.

I had also been taught that faith is a virtue and doubt is shameful and terrible. I recalled my humiliation when I had asked my first questions upon learning about the history of slavery in the United States. I certainly did not want to experience that again.

To entertain such thoughts and questions was a sin and displeasing to God. So, I fought these doubts rather than indulge them. I also had no one I could talk to about them for if I did, I would be responded to with anger and disappointment. We were to take God's word on faith, period. It was not our place to even question it.

This is the core of why it is so difficult for believers to turn from their beliefs. To ask evangelical Christians to even consider a piece of conflicting information you have presented equates, in their minds, to asking them to sin against God.

They won't openly think about contradictory information even if they were to reject it in the end because the very act of openly thinking about such information is an act of sin and shame. In order to change one's mind, one must first be open to the possibility that he/she is incorrect. But, for evangelical Christians, being so is simply against the rules.

I was instructed from a young age to guard my mind and heart and to take great care in what I allow to enter it. If information contradicted our faith, we were instructed to immediately run far away from it. Doing otherwise would displease God.

In children's church and Missionettes, we often sang a song about this, instilling this ideology early on.

> *Oh, be careful little eyes what you see*
> *Oh, be careful little eyes what you see*
> *For the father up above*
> *Is looking down in love*
> *So be careful little eyes what you see*
>
> *Oh, be careful little ears what you hear*
> *Oh, be careful little ears what you hear*
> *For the father up above*

Is looking down in love
So be careful little ears what you hear

In youth group, the instructions became much more graphic. If one of our eyes were to tempt us to stray from God's truth, we were to pluck it out. If one of our arms were to be a potential source of sin, we were to chop it off. It would be better to lose an eye or an arm than be damned to hell.

In other words, any part of ourselves that might even potentially turn our thoughts away from God (as he had been presented to us), that part of ourselves was to be immediately excised. Nothing about ourselves was significant, and we were to be willing to part with anything if it became necessary. Only God was significant.

For these reasons, in spite of these questions coming into my mind, I aggressively pushed them away and continued to pursue my faith. But, another seed of doubt had been planted. Its time to sprout and grow would someday come.

BIBLE COLLEGE AND THE MINISTRY

I enthusiastically loaded up my car with my meager belongings and headed to Bible college. I had finished high school and reached adulthood. I was thrilled.

It would have been difficult for the average person to guess that this was the case, however. The college I attended had very strict rules. Female students were required to wear dresses to class and chapel. Shorts were not allowed to be worn anywhere on campus. We could not leave overnight without prior permission.

We had a curfew. Women were not allowed in the mens dorms or vice versa, not even in the lobby areas. We were required to attend a pre-approved church every Sunday morning and evening. Chapel attendance was required, and we had a seating chart to insure our presence each weekday morning.

Students were not allowed to live off campus where their behavior and activity could not be easily monitored. Class attendance was mandatory. We could not exceed three absences each semester or we would receive a failing grade regardless of our performance on exams and assignments.

Students were kept in control as much as possible. It was not uncommon to hear of a fellow student's dismissal from the college for a failure to conform and comply. However, I was already well accustomed to rules and mandates, so I gave little thought to this arrangement.

BIBLE COLLEGE

The semester began, and I focused on my studies. Between chapel and church, I sat through seven services every single week. On top of that, I attended classes five days each week, most of which were about theology and the Bible. I was immersed in Biblical study.

They did offer (and require) two science courses. A significant portion of these two courses taught us how to refute evolutionary theory without ever teaching anything about the actual theory itself. We only needed to know that it was incorrect and baseless. I was elated to be studying science in a manner that was pleasing to God, and I believed the information taught to me in those science classes without question.

I did not care much for my other classes. Theology classes bored me. I did not want to learn different hypotheses about various deep, theological issues. I simply wanted to learn more about how to win the lost. I wanted to get out into the world and minister. I did not understand how these classes were going to assist me with doing so.

One consequence of these studies is that I began thinking more deeply about the stories in the Old Testament. My study of the Bible was now much more thorough and in depth, and approaching these stories in a more scholarly manner had cast them in a different light.

It was one thing to sit through a sermon at church and hear these stories presented in an inspiring manner. It was an entirely different experience to sit in a dry classroom lecture and dissect a story about a man building a boat that housed two of every single species on the face of the earth.

While I sat in chapel one day, a thought burst into my mind. What if these stories were not true? In a way, they sounded almost silly. What if they were basically no different than stories like Jack and the Beanstalk?

This revelation was jarring. A part of me seemed to understand that these stories did sound silly. A snake spoke to a woman in a garden while God was not looking.

A man was swallowed by a whale and hung out in there for three full days before being vomited onto a shore. For the first time, these stories sounded a little odd.

As clear and obvious as this may be for many people, it was too much for me to truly take in. God was real. The Bible was true. The alternative was just too unthinkable for me. I scolded myself for entertaining such a notion and dismissed it.

I refused to allow myself to think about such things further. Wondering such things displeased God. So, I pretended the questions were not there and pressed forward. Regardless, a third seed was planted deep in my mind that would wait for the opportune time to sprout.

Meanwhile, the yearning in my heart I had felt as a teenager remained. Something always felt slightly off, and I could never understand what it was.

I had hoped that at Bible college, I would finally elevate to the level I needed to be with God, causing this empty feeling in my heart to finally be filled. I considered also that perhaps this was simply part of living in a fallen world. Maybe none of us could truly be fully happy until we entered heaven.

If anyone had asked back then whether I was happy serving God, I would have said, without hesitation, that I absolutely was, and I would have meant it. Much of my life was happy. I experienced periods of extreme joy, especially during church services.

I truly believed I was happy and content. I just had this gnawing feeling deep in my heart that poked its head out here and there, and I did not understand what it was or why it would not go away. My proposed solutions always involved praying more, reading the Bible more, telling others about Jesus more, etc. It was never enough.

DATING

Life continued on. The summer prior to my junior year of college, I began dating a friend from high school who had converted to Christianity after our graduation. It was my first real relationship, and I was deeply in love with him.

We laughed the majority of the time we were together. He was witty and sarcastic, a type of humor I greatly enjoy. He helped me learn to take life less seriously. He taught me that it is ok to be silly for no other reason than to be silly and have fun.

Unfortunately, the relationship was doomed. While he had given faith the opportunity to prove itself, he was not convinced. He began to doubt the teachings of the church, and this placed a wedge between us.

I believed if I gave him time to pray and sort it out though, he would find his faith strengthened. So, I stood by him. After a year of dating, we were engaged to be married. This proved to reveal more differences between us than I had previously observed.

He had had sex with multiple people before converting to Christianity while I was not only a virgin, but hadn't even kissed anyone yet. He confidently and comfortably joked about sexual topics while I felt unsure and intimidated given my lack of experience.

We also had extreme political differences. Evangelical Christianity is not only a religious organization, but a political one. Supporting the Republican Party is preached from the pulpit on a regular basis and is considered the duty of all Christian people. To doubt this is to doubt God himself.

Evangelical preachers stand on the stage and scream about the evil liberals, describing them as wicked, godless people intent on eliminating God, destroying America, and murdering babies. They were demonic.

We demanded republican politicians. We insisted that prayer be mandatory in public schools. We accepted nothing less than basing every state and federal law on the Bible and our personal beliefs, and we believed that promoting the Republican Party was the way to make this happen.

My fiancé, being raised in a liberal household, held different views. He supported democratic politicians who, to me, were nothing but baby killers. He believed the church had no right to require other people to live by this faith. As we discussed these issues, I saw his mind was not changing, and the wedge between us pushed us further apart.

I desperately attempted to help him understand that America was a nation dedicated to God. Because of that dedication, God had blessed us with freedom and wealth. If we turned from his ways as a nation, God would withdraw his blessing. All hope would be lost. But, I could not persuade him.

His church attendance began to falter. He was losing interest, recognizing he did not fit there. I insisted he return to the fold and be the good, evangelical Christian he should be. When it became clear he was not going to do so, we ended the relationship.

I had been shopping for my wedding dress and planning our lives together. My heart was utterly shattered. The only comfort I found was the belief that God would reward me for making the right decision. I had to put God first, and I could not be bound to someone without a strong faith. Through my tears, I firmly believed that in time, God would bring me peace.

ARRIVAL

As I waited for that peace to come, I focused on my senior year of Bible college. It passed rather quickly while I completed an internship at a local church. Before I knew it, I was graduating.

My parents, family, and friends were wonderfully proud of me. I walked across the stage in sheer exhilaration. It had been a very long journey. Bible college is not easy. It took a lot of work.

There were times it seemed I would never finish. But, I did. I received my degree, a symbol of my accomplishment, and I was exceedingly happy. I thought back to the first moment when I accepted God's call and reflected on all of the obstacles I had faced to reach this point. I had arrived. I was going into the ministry. It was finally happening.

I was bursting with excitement as I envisioned what lay ahead. I had already been offered my first position at a church as an associate minister. I had been hired to initiate and oversee the church's outreach efforts. We were going to build a trailer that would work as a stage.

This trailer would be driven to the various neighborhoods throughout the city, bringing church to those who had not yet found God. I imagined all the children and families I would get to know and be able to help. My heart was full. I could not wait to begin. I was ready.

But, things are not always as they seem.

MINISTRY

The ministry soon revealed much of the inner workings of the church to which before, I had not been privy. I observed extraordinary amounts of conflict. I saw many people, both ministers and lay people, vying for power and control.

I had no interest in such matters. I simply wanted to work with families and support them on their journey with God. I was surprised at how difficult that was to do in the ministry. The building of the trailer was delayed repeatedly due to, I was told, a lack of funding.

There always seemed to be money to spend on fixing up the building to keep it in pristine condition, but there was never funding for outreach to areas affected by poverty and various forms of social injustice. Not one dollar was ever spent on those efforts during my time there.

To give me something to do, I was assigned the task of teaching children's church on Sunday mornings. It's not that I did not enjoy doing so. I did. But, that was not what this position was supposed to revolve around.

During the many sermons I had listened to since childhood, I had been taught that our focus was to be on building the Kingdom of God. We were to be leading the lost to the Lord. We were to care for the poor and destitute. We were to bring healing to the sick.

We were to bring deliverance to the addicted. I took these instructions very seriously. That is what I went into the ministry to do, but attempting to do so through the church was an impossible task.

Witnessing the conversations that surrounded important decisions was absolutely shocking. It became clear that the church was working very hard to invite white, wealthy people who were leaving one church and desiring to join another.

When I suggested programs that would reach the lost outside of our church walls, I was always immediately shot down. Think of the wear and tear on the building if we brought in children on a bus. Think of the upkeep of a trailer to bring the church to people living in poverty-stricken areas. It was not practical.

However, there was always money for lavish musicals and famous Christian singers to draw in the right kind of crowd. I continued to wait for the church to set aside some funding in the budget for outreach. That time would never come.

After two years, one of the associate ministers turned on the senior pastor at the church. He spread several lies to a few members of the board and to key congregation members. The conflict grew worse and worse until the senior pastor finally resigned and left.

It was clear that the true position I had desired at this church would never become reality, so I began seeking a position elsewhere. This is not an easy process for a female minister.

While women were considered able to be ordained ministers in my denomination, that amounted to little more than a statement in the by-laws. Most churches, when seeking to fill a ministry position, listed under the required qualifications, "Married male."

For the most part, the only churches that did not include this in the required qualifications were churches that wanted or needed to fill a position for an extremely low salary. The ministry in evangelical Christianity surely holds the greatest inequality of wages based on gender of any field of employment.

After some searching and interviews, I accepted a position half way across the country that paid a salary of $800 per month. The senior pastor at this church seemed focused on outreach when we spoke, which excited me. But, when I arrived, I found much was the same as the church I had just left.

Efforts to grow the congregation to a greater number centered around events that would draw white, wealthy people and encourage them to leave their current church and join ours. A child began to attend church on his own initiative from the neighborhood. He was from a difficult home situation, so I invested some time into him to support and encourage him.

My pastor stepped in and stated that his parents were not going to join the church and become tithing members, so my energies were better spent elsewhere. The goal, he explained, was to increase the congregation so we could build a new sanctuary. He instructed me to stop investing time with that child because that child was not going to help us reach this goal.

I was experiencing enormous frustration. As time passed, I became more and more disillusioned. I was forced to serve a building rather than God. I wanted out.

Making matters worse, throughout all this time, that lingering, gnawing feeling in my heart continued to torment me. At the time, it helped that I finally had something to blame. I wasn't fulfilling my calling to God because the churches I worked for created so many barriers to doing so. I had to find a way to overcome those barriers.

I tried so hard. My efforts accomplished nothing. Once, at an event held by the district of my denomination, I attended a talk that was for the wives of ministers. I was not a wife of a minister, but since all the women were going to it and the men were going to a different talk, I went with the women.

Even at a district event for ministers, I fit no where. A woman stood before us and spoke about the confusion we can sometimes feel about what God must be up to. She assured us, though, that our steps were ordered of God. All of us were right where God desired for us to be.

I had tears in my eyes. Nothing had gone the way I had imagined since I entered the ministry. Could it be that I was still right where God wanted me to be and doing what God wanted me to be doing? The thought gave me assurance that perhaps I could continue this after all. Her words provided a shining ray of hope during that dark night.

She gave each of us a knick knack shaped like a high-heeled shoe to serve as a reminder to us that God orders our steps. I set it on my dresser at home and cherished it. It gave me the strength I needed to carry on just a little further.

CHANGE

The final year that I was in ministry, I was miserable. I had become overwhelmed with debt as I was awfully underpaid, making less than the poverty level (while my senior pastor was paid eleven times my salary). I felt I was working so hard to do little more than maintain a pretty church building to attract those considered worthy of attending.

Something had to change. But, I felt trapped. What else could I do? I could not get another job with nothing more than a degree from an unaccredited Bible college.

I prayed for direction. Should I go to yet another church and see if I could find the right place for me? Maybe I had just had some bad luck and ended up in a couple of terrible churches. The thought of struggling to find a position yet again, due to my gender and marital status, was daunting.

Then, one night, seemingly out of the blue, I had an epiphany. I could return to school and study psychology. After that, I could become a Christian counselor. It would be a different type of ministry, but it would give me freedom that my current position didn't allow.

The intensity of my excitement surpassed anything I had felt in a long time. The more I thought about it, the more I could not wait. I immediately and eagerly began researching the different options to pursue a degree that would allow me to do this. However, I quickly ran into a serious problem.

Because I already had a college degree, I could not receive financial aid outside of loans. But, because I had attended a college that was not accredited, I would be required to complete a full 4-year degree all over again since none of my credits would transfer.

I was crushed. I felt so defeated. When I was in youth group, it was pressed upon us that attending this particular Bible college was vital. There was no need to get a second major or attend an accredited university.

We were told to trust God and place it all into his hands. We were to live by faith. He would see to it that we were provided for. Pursuing a second major or attending an accredited college would be a sign of a lack of faith. Why would we need a back-up major if we were planning on God providing for us while in ministry?

Now, here I sat in front of the computer learning how much this advice had harmed me. After taking a few days to consider my dilemma, I decided to incur the debt and attend school. While this option was far from ideal, my other, limited options were even worse.

I enrolled in two online classes to begin while continuing my ministry position. One was a statistics course that was an important prerequisite for other courses I would need to take later. The other was a class called Brain and Behavior.

The description of the class intrigued me. I had always been fascinated by the connection between the biology of the brain and human behavior. I knew very little about it since I had all but written off science from my life. But, my curiosity occasionally piqued as I would watch a documentary on TV or read an article in a magazine.

I expected that I would learn about the beauty and magnificence of God's design in this class. I was certain that I would see God's work in every piece of information I learned. I could not have been more incorrect.

What I was about to learn would slowly and irreversibly change the course of my life and my perception of the world. Soon, those seeds of doubt I had buried so deeply years before would receive some water. The soil would become more fertile. Those seeds were about to sprout and grow.

REVELATIONS

My Brain and Behavior class was underway. Because I was still in ministry, I had enrolled in online courses to accommodate my work schedule. I had an online classroom that I visited frequently.

I was assigned specific chapters to read from my textbooks each week. I had papers to write. I had exams to prepare for. And I was glowing.

The information in those pages was absolutely thrilling to read. Lights of joy were suddenly switched on in my heart as I turned the pages. I was fascinated. I began by learning about the general parts of the nervous system and then, about the four lobes of the brain and an overview of each.

The frontal lobe, as its name indicates, sits at the front of the human brain. Our cognitive functions and control of movement happen here. Behind the frontal lobe sits the parietal lobe, responsible for processing information about temperature, taste, touch, and movement.

Moving downward, we find the temporal lobe where our memories are processed and stored. This lobe also processes auditory stimuli and is necessary for language and speech.

Finally, at the back of the human brain sits the occipital lobe where information related to vision is processed.

We moved deeper. I studied images of the brain as I learned to identify the various parts. The amygdala, the cerebellum, the hippocampus, the hypothalamus…it was all there, waiting for me to discover in those pages.

As I moved further into the semester, I experienced a significant transformation. To my astonishment, the nagging feeling of emptiness that had walked with me all those years began to fade. A fullness and satisfaction illuminated the core of my being. For the very first time, I felt as though I had found my place.

SCIENCE

I devoured the information, learning much more than the class required, and I quickly came to notice a disturbing reality. The field of science as a whole was quite different than the description that had been presented to me from a young age.

I had heard repeatedly, in both conversations and sermons from the pulpit, that people who follow science do so without thought. Scientists arrogantly stand and declare what they believed to be true and demand that others agree. Their followers, particularly students at universities, swallow the information whole without question and are led astray.

This scenario was not at all what I observed in my studies. I never had information declared to me as true with the expectation of it being believed without question. Each piece of information offered in my textbooks was consistently followed by a summary of its supporting evidence (the reference list for one of my textbooks filled 53 full textbook-sized pages).

We were encouraged to question. We were encouraged to

doubt. We were invited to share contradictory or alternative ideas as long as we had adequate data to support our claims. No one stood anywhere in this field demanding belief without critical thought. On the contrary, critical thought is what was demanded of us more than anything else.

This discovery shook me and the very foundation on which I stood. Everyone I had ever trusted as an authority had emphatically insisted that the field of science was a specific way, but I had just learned, by observing this field with my own eyes, that they were wrong. What they had been wrong about was no small issue for me.

I had been made to feel so ashamed of myself for finding science enjoyable when it was supposedly such an evil, devious field. I had felt filthy and dirty as a result of my love for science. Those terrible feelings had then led me to make some significant decisions about my life.

I had stopped studying science. I had turned away from its allure because I had believed it was filled with deceit and arrogance. I could now see that was not true. Perhaps there was never a real reason to have turned from science in the first place.

I began to wrestle with what this could mean. If they had been wrong about this, what else had they been wrong about? Maybe it was the preachers, rather than the scientists, who were actually leading people astray.

I was not questioning my actual faith at this time. But, my confidence in the knowledge of the leaders of my faith was greatly shaken. More significantly, my confidence in my own knowledge was destroyed. I realized I did not know nearly as much as I had thought I did.

I had believed for years that scientists were conceited and arrogant and that they insisted they knew everything there was to know. I could now see that it was I who had been conceited and arrogant. I had thought I had all the answers. I had made decisions about people and about entire fields of knowledge before even giving them the chance.

The world no longer seemed simple. Life was no longer black and white. This was hugely problematic for me because evangelical Christianity requires binary thinking. It is an all or nothing proposition.

You either devote all of your life to God, every single minute detail, or you have devoted none of it. The Bible is 100% true and all other religious texts are 100% false. Conservatives are sincere and godly, and liberals are malevolent and vile. To function in evangelical Christianity, black and white, binary thinking is a must.

Yet, these scientists, always described to me as foolish, godless, immoral soldiers of the devil, were not foolish, malevolent, or dishonest. Perhaps they were not led by God, but they were not devious, either. They did not fit into my "good versus evil" perspective of the world.

As I learned more about the nervous system, the brain, and their many complexities, the world became even more grey rather than black and white. My own binary thinking was beginning to crumble.

NEURONS

Our nervous system contains billions of cells called neurons. They "work" by receiving and sending messages.

Visualize a circular cell. Now, imagine that cell has lots of small tree branches extending from all around it with the exception of one small area. These extensions are called dendrites.

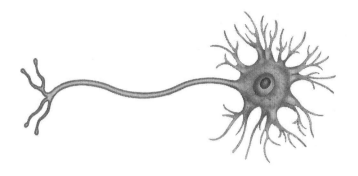

Now, imagine a long, noodle-shaped appendage protruding from the small area of the cell that lacks extending dendrites. This is called an axon. Together, the axon, dendrites, and the bulb containing the nucleus and various organelles compose a neuron (organelles are to a cell what organs are to your body).

If we wanted to build a neural circuit, a pathway of communication in the brain and/or nervous system, we would lay neurons down and connect them to one another. Let's pretend neurons are the size of your arm. You pick one up and lay it down. Now, pick up another. The second neuron's dendrites will be placed next to the end of the axon of the first.

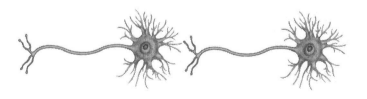

The dendrites of one neuron and the axon of another do

not actually touch. There is a very tiny gap, called a synaptic gap, between them. Still, they are connected to one another via the synaptic gap. To continue the circuit, a third neuron should be placed with its dendrites next to the axon of the second. And so forth.

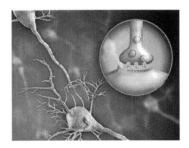

Everything I describe next is a bit of an oversimplification. If you desire to know more details about the process I am about to describe, I have included a section in the appendix dedicated to this purpose.

I had been led to believe that our thoughts were part of our mind or soul, something completely separate from the brain. The reasoning was that biology alone could not produce consciousness. The brain could not possibly contain thought. In this class, I learned how messages travel through the brain entirely through physical, biological processes.

To send a message, the end of an axon releases a neurotransmitter into the synaptic gap between it and its neighboring cells' dendrites. These dendrites have receptors for those particular neurotransmitters. When enough of that neurotransmitter binds to receptors on the dendrites of a neighboring cell, that neighboring cell opens doors at the top of its axon.

When it does, sodium ions surrounding the cell rush in through some of the doors while potassium ions rush out of the other doors. This ignites similar doors to open a little further down the axon with the same result. Sodium ions rush in and potassium ions rush out.

This then opens doors even further down the axon. And so on and so forth all the way to the end of the axon. Through this means, what is called an action potential travels down the axon.

When the action potential reaches the end of the axon, a neurotransmitter is released from the axon and into the synaptic gap to bind to the dendrites of neighboring cells, and the process begins again in those neurons.

This process is happening in billions of neurons within your brain right now as you read this book. Through this magnificent symphony, we experience sensation, emotion, thought, reason, and more.

THE SOUL?

I had long heard that messages travel from brain cell to brain cell and down nerves to muscles to tell them to move and so forth. I assumed that scientists did not know what that message was, meaning they did not know exactly what was traveling across those cells.

I believed those messages were part of our mind or soul and that they could not be quantified or observed in the physical realm. Now, I realized that they actually did know what was traveling across the cells. They even knew how it was traveling across the cells. It could be and had been quantified and observed.

As I delved deeper, I considered a significant implication that, for me, was life altering. If this process was so clearly a fully biological process, how did the concept of the soul fit into all of this?

My entire life, I had believed that the soul of an individual was who that person really was. The mind and the soul were separate from the body. The mortal body was just a shell, housing the real us, which was immortal.

But, if our thoughts and memories were all contained in our physical brain rather than within a magical goo floating in or around us, what were the mind and soul? Was the mind just a word to describe the experience of consciousness that occurs entirely within our biological brains? How could we travel to heaven after death, leaving our brains behind and still retain our personalities, experiences, and perceptions?

As I learned more and more about the brain, I saw no hint that a soul was necessary for it to function properly. There was no sign of a spiritual connection at all. The basics were explained through natural, physical means.

While the implications of this were there in my thoughts, I could only indulge them to a small degree. When a person spends years within the evangelical Christian faith, it consumes every part of his/her identity.

In spite of what I had come to see, the information I had just learned was asking me to disregard all I had come to know about myself, my life, and the world. I was being asked to give up the deeply personal and intimate God who had been my closest friend for many years.

These processes take lots of time if they ever even happen at all. Thus, in spite of these questions I wondered about, I continued to pursue my faith, assuming I would eventually find a way to explain it all and make things work. I had simply hit a bump in the road. Surely, everything would be alright.

STATISTICS

I cannot say I was equally as fascinated while taking my statistics course compared to my Brain and Behavior course.

Still, I learned information even in that course that cast my beliefs in a different light.

Throughout my life, I had frequently heard a statement that provided an excuse to dismiss science outright: "Statistics can be made to say whatever we want them to say."

Note that this statement is spoken not only inside evangelical Christianity. Even many secular people believe this to be true. However, in religion, it is used as an excuse to disregard any data or discovery that contradicts one's faith.

Indeed, statistics performed improperly can be twisted around and forced to conform to an incorrect claim. But, real statistical analyses, properly done, cannot be used for such purposes. When we correctly conduct a statistical analysis, the answer is simply the answer. We can accept it or be wrong.

For example, suppose I had a data set collected on two groups of organisms and that data had been collected properly. There is a simple, statistical analysis called a t-test I could perform. The t-test would tell me one of two things about any differences between the groups that were observed and measured in my experiment.

The t-test would tell me that any differences between the two groups were likely just a coincidence, or it would tell me that those differences had an extremely low probability of occurring due to chance. If it turned out to be the latter, it would be very likely that the differences between the two groups were due to what I had done in the experiment since the odds of them being a coincidence were exceptionally low.

After we submit the data to a t-test, it will giver us a value, which we call a p-value. A p-value of .05 means there is a 5% chance that the difference between two groups is just a coincidence. If a p-value is .01, that means there is a 1% chance that the difference is merely coincidental.

A researcher will get really excited if the p-value is .001 or even less as this means there is only a .01% chance that the difference is a coincidence. In this case, the chances that the difference was caused by the independent variable, the variable controlled by the researchers, is quite high.

For example, suppose we are testing a new drug. We get a large group of people living with the condition this medication is intended to treat. We split them up randomly. It is important that this is done randomly because if you have a large enough group, randomly placing members into one of two groups means other unique variables will be spread out evenly amongst the two groups.

For example, the racial and gender composition of each group will be similar. Disease severity will not be the same in each individual, but it will be the same overall when each total group is compared to the other total group. And so forth.

One group is given the medication while the other group is given a placebo, meaning they are given something that looks like the medication, but isn't and that is known to have a benign affect on the condition of study. In this case, the medication is the independent variable. That is the one difference between these two groups when the study begins.

Each of these individuals then have data collected regarding their disease status. Those collecting the data do not know which individuals are receiving the medication and which individuals are receiving the placebo. This removes the chance of the data being collected in a biased way, even if the person does not mean to be biased and would only impact the data inadvertently.

The study is done and the data set is complete. Prior to running the statistical analysis (in this example, a t-test), the researchers decide which value of p it must be under in order to determine their hypothesis is correct. In medicine, choosing a value of .01 is typical. Thus, the researchers decide if the p-value is less than .01, the medication works. Then, they conduct the statistical analysis to see what the p-value is.

There are other ways to design scientific studies, and there are many different statistical analyses (which one will be used depends on the type of data that is being analyzed). What became clear to me through this course was that scientists cannot simply come up with numbers through some willy nilly process and make the data say whatever they desire.

Properly done science yields an answer that is out of our control. The answer is simply the answer. We can embrace it and adjust our knowledge to accommodate it, or we can deny it and be wrong.

I saw once again that science was not a field of inquiry wrought with dishonesty and deceit like I had been told. Integrity, caution, care, and critical thought were foundational components of the entire field.

Scientists did not just make stuff up. They did not twist around numbers to say whatever they wished. I had spent years believing that scientists fabricate data and cheat in order to trick people into becoming atheists. I had been told this many times since I was very young. I could now see this was completely untrue.

I was struggling for sure. But, at the same time, I firmly believed I would find a way to reconcile this knowledge and affirm my faith. However, things were about to get a lot more complicated.

As the semester progressed and I continued to learn about the human brain and how it worked, I would learn more and more information that would cast my faith in a different light. The point of no return was much closer than I understood.

THE MIND

While I remained unsure of how to adequately coordinate these new discoveries with my faith, I continued in ministry. Everything felt different. I listened to my senior pastor on Sundays with an absence of confidence in his knowledge. I found my thoughts wandering from the service and toward questions I had about issues that were, to me, much more urgent.

I continued to wonder how the concept of the soul fit into what I was learning.

DUALISM

I had been raised to be a dualist. Dualism is a belief that the mind and body are each composed of completely different substances that interact with one another. One famous dualist, though certainly not the first, was Rene' Descartes. He proposed that the body was essentially a machine made of the substance of earth. The mind, on the other hand, was made of some kind of magical goo.

The body was responsible for the digestion of food,

breathing, sleeping, and other such biological functions while the mind/magical goo was responsible for thinking, feeling, and making decisions. He also suggested that the body collects the sensory stimuli surrounding us and transmits it to the pineal gland, a small structure in the brain.

He believed the pineal gland is where the magical goo and the body meet together to exchange information. The mind receives the information about the physical environment there and it then communicates its directions to the body there as well. Descartes intended to prove, through evidence, that this idea was correct. Not surprisingly, he failed to do so, never offering a single piece of evidence to support his claim.

While his idea may sound silly, I was essentially believing something similar and a significant percentage of people around the world still do. If we are part magical goo and part a physical body, where and how do they interact to exchange information with one another? In order to adequately claim that these two different substances exist, this question must be answered.

In fact, scientists have attempted to answer this very question. Many have tried to locate an area of the brain to which all information funnels in order to be brought together into one place and produce our singular experience of consciousness or the "little person in the head," so to speak. Nothing that even remotely resembles this has ever been found.

There is another question that must be answered by dualists. If our thoughts, feelings, and decisions are taking place in the magical goo, why is it that components of our physical body, especially the brain, appear to not only influence our magical goo, but even exert control over it?

If we lose parts of the brain, we lose parts of the mind. If we stimulate parts of the brain, we can directly influence thoughts, experiences, and behavior. Have you ever gotten drunk and said things you later regretted? Or have you at least known someone who has done so?

Alcohol decreases our inhibitions, and it does so in multiple ways. It decreases the flow of sodium across membranes which, in turn, results in a decrease in serotonin. It also blocks specific receptors on neurons.

These changes result in a feeling of pleasure and a decrease in inhibitions. If our thoughts and decisions occur in the magical goo, then, drinking alcohol should not impact our decision-making. Yet, it does.

I once asked about this issue to an evangelical Christian friend of mine. Her response was, "Well, that is why you should not drink alcohol."

This, of course, in no way answered the question posed. I began to notice when I asked questions like these as I tried to find my way through them, the typical evangelical Christian response was to simply change the subject. The answers I received were not only unsatisfying, they were answers that did not even address the question in the first place.

Alcohol is not the only example to give regarding physical changes influencing our thoughts. There are many, many more. Let's go over just a couple more.

DAMAGE TO THE BRAIN

I learned about two individuals who experienced damage to the prefrontal cortex during infancy that were observed. From early in their lives all the way into adulthood, they routinely made terrible decisions and appeared to have no understanding of moral behavior. They frequently lied, stole, and physically and verbally abused others. They showed no signs of guilt at any time. They were unable to maintain friendships or hold a job in spite of having a normal IQ.

I learned of another man who endured similar damage to

his prefrontal cortex later in life as an adult. He lost his ability to feel emotion. Because of this, he was incapable of making appropriate decisions. He was perfectly competent when predicting the possible outcomes of different choices in any given situation (approval of friends for one option vs disapproval of friends for the other option or getting into trouble for one option vs getting rewarded for another option, etc).

Yet, even after describing those potential consequences, he was unable to identify which choice would be better for him. He could not understand whether a consequence of happiness was better or worse than a consequence of sadness. It was as though his brain simply could not compute such information anymore, so he was unable to make such determinations. He lost his job, quickly burned through his savings, and his marriage fell apart.

How do these people fit into the scope of a soul that will be punished or rewarded for the decisions it makes if they lack the ability to control and fully understand their decisions? How do any of us? I began to wonder, "how much control over our decisions does our consciousness actually have?"

Most of us have never suffered traumatic brain injury, but our brains are a little different for each of us as a result of our individual DNA and experiences we have had in life. One person's ability to assess outcomes of a decision will be greater than someone else's due to circumstances neither of those people had a say in.

A man who endured brain damage subsequently suffered epileptic activity (increased activity) in the temporal lobes of his cerebral cortex. He began to demonstrate outbursts of violence and rage, often attacking his wife, physically. Many treatments were tried, but all of them failed.

Finally, desperate for a solution, he agreed to have a

surgical procedure during which a small part of the amygdala in his brain was destroyed. Stimulation of the amygdala in animals is strongly associated with attack behaviors. The hope was that this procedure would reduce his tendency toward violence. The surgery was a success, and the episodes of violence and rage ceased.

The lessons here are important. A person who did not desire to harm his wife and had no previous history of aggression toward her became incapable of not harming his wife when a small area of his brain became overactive.

What about people who, due to genetic and/or environmental reasons, have heightened activity in the amygdala in their brains? How responsible for their behavior are their minds or magical goo if they attack someone?

We do not have the full answers to these questions. What we do know, however, is that biological differences in the brain impact our ability to make decisions, to feel, and to even think. If the mind or soul is a separate entity from the body, this should not be true.

If there is a God who rewards or punishes us for our decisions with eternal paradise or eternal torture, surely, a basic requirement for such a system would be that each individual, a soul, has complete and utter control over his/her decisions. Otherwise, this God would be nightmarishly unjust and cruel.

The more I learned, the more it appeared that we are not made of two separate materials with a mind or a soul. The mind, as we call it, seemed to simply be a metaphor for our experience of consciousness.

Everything we know suggests that we are physical, not spiritual, beings.

EVOLUTIONARY THEORY

While it was not a central component of the course, we did cover a section about the basics of evolutionary theory. Remember, I was a creationist when I opened that book. I had been led to believe that evolution was a baseless and ridiculous theory advanced by evil, atheist scientists who were hell bent on destroying God and leading the world astray.

I had also been taught that there was a lot of controversy surrounding evolutionary theory and that it was not well accepted in the scientific community. I was firmly told there was a lot of disagreement in the scientific community about whether we evolved. Ironically, I did not realize until much later how contradictory the statements in this paragraph and the prior paragraph are.

We will get into evolutionary theory a bit deeper in a later chapter. I did not learn much about evolution in this class. What struck me, though, was the fact that in the class, we were taught that one cannot study any field of biology without having at least a foundational understanding of evolutionary theory.

I discovered that there is no big controversy surrounding evolutionary theory in the scientific community. It is well accepted there. Scientists are not debating creationism verses evolution. What I had been told was wrong.

Evolution is the backbone of biology, the professor stated. One could not understand who we are today as a species without first understanding where our species has been. As the semester progressed, I learned about various human behaviors and little quirks we have that are evolutionary remnants of our species' past.

In other words, we have traits that were once useful to

one of our ancestor species. The genes for those traits had not yet faded out completely.

One simple example is the fact that we get goosebumps. Goosebumps serve us no purpose, yet we still get them. Our hairier ancestors did have a use for them, though. In certain settings, goosebumps would raise their hair, which served as an advantage for them.

We do not have enough hair to raise in such a manner, yet we still get goosebumps under certain circumstances. They're an evolutionary remnant. Many species have such remnants.

I did not fully understand evolutionary theory. Still, what I was learning made sense. But, I had been told evolutionary theory did not make sense in any way. This confused and perplexed me.

If evolutionary theory was without evidence, why would the vast majority of scientists accept it as true? What I had seen so far in my studies was that scientists require evidence before they will agree with a claim. Thus, if essentially the entire field of science, especially the field of biological science, understood evolutionary theory to be true, one could surmise there was plenty of strong evidence for it.

But, how could that be? I had been taught that evolutionary theory was stupid and made up. Had the people I trusted and looked to for truth been wrong about that, too?

I was about to learn even more, and things were going to change quite a bit for me.

SEXUAL ORIENTATION

If you ask a typical evangelical Christian, he/she will tell you that in God's eyes, all sin is equal. Sin is sin. However, if you then observed that evangelical Christian's behavior, you would likely witness behaviors that strongly suggest that he or she believes otherwise.

I recall an evangelical Christian telling me once, after she'd just returned home from the grocery store, that she saw a lesbian couple shopping for groceries. She needed something that was in the aisle in which they were shopping. Rather than simply walking down the aisle to get what she needed, she went to the next aisle and secretly waited until they left. She then proceeded to continue her shopping, unabated by the presence of lesbians.

I dare say this same individual would not have hid in a neighboring aisle if she had seen a heterosexual couple who had chosen to not wait for marriage to have sex. I would bet dimes to donuts that she would not have similarly responded to the presence of an obese individual, either.

Why do I mention obesity? It is not from a place of judgment toward anyone struggling with being overweight. Trust me, I am in no place to pass judgment. Gluttony, however, or eating in excess, the cause behind the explosion of obesity in our modern society, is declared in the Bible to be a sin. Yet, it is an almost celebrated act in the average evangelical church.

It is not an unusual event for parishioners to attend the Sunday morning service and pray to God in efforts to keep themselves pure and free from sin. Then, they immediately leave the house of God and together, head to the buffet to gorge themselves for their Sunday dinner.

This sin, apparently, is not so bad. But, woe to the homosexual who commits the greatest of sins. There will be weeping and gnashing of teeth waiting for them in the fires of eternal torment.

My entire life, or since I knew that gay people existed, I had believed that homosexuals chose to be homosexuals as a means of rebelling against God. I believed this because I had been taught to believe this. And it is no wonder why this had been taught to me.

To accept that homosexuality is worthy of eternal damnation, it certainly should be a choice a person makes. What kind of God would create people to be homosexuals and then, punish them for being so? The idea that sexual orientation is a choice is a necessity for believing one deserves punishment for it.

However, I was about to learn some information that would shatter what I had once believed about sexual orientation. So far, I had been led to believe that homosexuality was an abomination. It was perverse, and it enraged God and disgusted him. It was unnatural, literally the complete and utter opposite of nature. It opposed God's plan in every way a plan could be opposed.

I was shocked as I turned the pages in my textbook and learned that homosexuality has been observed in many different species in the natural world. We have observed it in pigs. We have observed it in goats. We have observed it in finches. We have observed it in rats.

Could a rat truly consider its creator, choose to rebel, and opt for homosexuality? The thought was absurd.

Further, there were a number of studies through which investigators increased the chance a rat would be homosexual by exposing a pregnant rat to extreme stress for two hours daily (we could discuss the ethics surrounding putting an animal through this, but that is a subject for another book). Rats born to such females had a significantly higher chance of being homosexuals.

If we could increase the chance that a baby rat would be born gay, what did that mean for us? This does not mean that people are homosexual because their mothers were stressed during pregnancy. Rats and humans are not the same species.

However, it did show that rats do not decide to be homosexual.

Neither do goats. Neither do pigs. Neither do finches. Whether through the same means or through entirely different pathways in each species, we have observed that animals are born gay.

If homosexuality is so unnatural, why would animals living in nature be born gay? If God is so appalled by homosexuality, why would he create homosexual animals? Lastly, if animals were gay without choosing to be so, doesn't this mean it was possible human beings are also gay without choosing to be so?

I further read that studies showed that identical twins were most likely to share their sexual orientation. If one identical twin is gay, there is not 100% chance his identical twin will be gay, but the chance that he will be is significantly higher when compared to the general population.

Non-identical twins are not as likely to share sexual orientation as identical twins, but still much more likely than non-twin brothers and sisters who, in turn, are more likely to share sexual orientation than brothers and sisters who were adopted and from separate biological families.

This has been studied enough times that it is clear that while genes do not provide the entire answer, there is most certainly a genetic component to sexual orientation. As I thought about this, I realized I had never made the decision to be straight.

There was no point in my life in which I felt I could go either way and opted to go with heterosexuality for the purposes of pleasing Jesus. I am simply attracted to men and that is just the way I am. I can't fathom ever being sexually attracted to a woman.

And then, it dawned on me. What if gay people felt the same way? What if a gay man was attracted to men because he simply was and he, too, could not fathom ever being sexually attracted to a woman? What if a lesbian could not fathom ever being sexually attracted to a man?

Gay people suddenly did not seem so different from me. They no longer seemed disgusting or unnatural. But, how could I accept such an idea? Homosexuality had clearly been demonstrated to me as being one of the worst sins a person could commit.

All of this made God appear to be appallingly unjust. I thought about the first openly gay person I had ever met. It was in high school. I will call her T. T was open about being a lesbian.

One day, two of my church friends and I were walking into the mall, and we saw T in the distance across the parking lot. I mentioned that she was gay. We then noticed that she was walking with another girl. We all three looked at each other and made sounds of utter disgust as we laughed and mocked her from afar.

As I recalled this memory, I felt incredibly ashamed. I remembered that the following year, I sat behind T in an English class, and I got to know her a little bit. She was very friendly and kind. There was nothing about her worthy of the disgust my friends and I had bestowed upon her that day at the mall.

As I pondered all I had learned from this class, I considered T. She was fun. I had enjoyed getting to know her. I realized she did not choose to be gay. She simply was. Why did it really matter? She was not hurting anyone. Nothing about her made it seem reasonable for her to be deserving of eternal torture.

I reflected on all of the statements this made about God and my faith. I did not know how to reconcile any of this. As I struggled to make sense of all I had learned, I had no idea just how quickly and drastically things were about to change.

DEEPENING QUESTIONS

I was incredibly distraught. I felt my faith beginning to falter, and that terrified me. I needed answers, and it became clear I would not be able to find these answers on my own. I had to ask for the input of others.

I approached a member of my family and mentioned that I had come to learn that homosexuals do not choose to be homosexuals. They simply are. I asked, "So, how can God punish them for being gay?"

He replied, "Well, it's ok if someone is born gay. That doesn't mean homosexual relationships are not sinful. It's because of the curse. We are all born with a desire to sin, and certain sins will be more appealing to us than others. For some people, that sin is homosexuality."

That satisfied me for the moment. However, that night, as I waited to fall asleep, I contemplated this more. I thought about the curse. I wondered why I should be born cursed as a result of a sin committed by someone thousands of years ago when I did not even exist.

Why should I be held responsible for the sin of someone

else? In what way did that make me or anyone else deserving of a curse?

I then recalled a conversation I had had several years before with a family who were dear friends of mine. The husband in the family stated that his children will have an easier life because they came from multiple generations of godly men and women. He then implied that the path will be more difficult for me since my parents were the first to convert to our religion.

He explained that the sins of the fathers are visited onto his children and his children's children. The Bible does indeed say this. He was not making that up. He said that likewise, God visits the blessings of the fathers onto his children and his children's children as well.

I was shocked and appalled. I said, "Why should I have it harder and your son have it easier over something we did not even do and were not even here for? What my great grandfather was doing had nothing to do with me."

He insisted that the Bible told us this is true and therefore, it is right, it is just, and it must be believed. That never did sit right with me, though I had not thought too deeply about it. But, that night, as I lay in bed, I did think deeply about it.

THE IMPLICATIONS

In our society, we acknowledge there will be some inherent unfairness based on who we are born to. Someone born into poverty will face many obstacles that will not be faced by someone born into wealth. However, we at least try to even the playing field a bit. We have college grants that are greater in their amounts for those from families with less income than those from families with more income.

We have free school lunches for children from families below the poverty level to be sure children from poor families do not have the disadvantage of going all day without a meal while their wealthier peers need not worry about such things.

When a parent is convicted of a crime and sentenced to jail, we would never tolerate a judge sending the parent's child to jail as well. On the contrary, there are many charity organizations aimed to help children who currently have a parent incarcerated to help them cope with that reality. We don't punish children for the wrongdoings of their parents. We help the children in these situations.

We, as fallible, feeble people understood that it is not fair to make a child suffer because of the actions of the person to whom the child was born. Did God not understand this? How could this be fair or just?

Why should I be born into sin and depravity because someone else listened to a snake and ate from the tree of knowledge? How could I possibly deserve to be punished for something someone else did?

As I wrestled with these thoughts, a feeling of terror washed over me. I recalled quite suddenly that it was not our place to question God. If I did question too much, what if I lost my faith? What would happen to me then?

I had been told exactly what would happen to me were that to ever happen. I had been told it from a young age, but one particular evening in youth group, when I was about 15 years old, had impacted me the most.

One night, during Wednesday night youth service, we were told the service would be outdoors surrounding a giant bonfire. We sat around it, mesmerized. It easily burned 15 feet above the ground. We could not get very close as it was too hot to tolerate. Our youth pastor instructed us to get as close to the fire as we could without being scorched and to sit there so we could feel its radiating heat.

He stood before us and preached a sermon about hell. As we felt the heat from the flames, he told us to imagine what it would be like for someone to pick us up and cast us into the fire. Imagine how it would feel. Imagine the pain and torment. It would be a horrifying and agonizing way to die.

Now, we were to imagine hell. In hell, no one dies. Those who are there are already dead. The burning and excruciating pain would have no end ever. We could cry out in agony every moment, screaming for the slightest relief, but it would never come. Trillions of years would pass, and still, we would burn.

It was a frightening sermon. I did imagine being thrust into those flames as I felt their heat reach my skin. My hands shook as I worked to fathom the indescribable torture that I would endure were I to ever enter hell. The concept of hell was made quite real to me that evening, and I was horrified.

Now, as an adult, I recalled the sensation from that heat and the accompanying fright. I wondered if the questions I was asking would lead me to hell. I was struggling to believe. How far could these struggles go before I lost my salvation?

I was reminded of how often we were told to be careful what we allow into our minds and hearts for there were many things in this world that could lead us astray if we were not careful. Perhaps this was the warning about what scientific study would do to me. After all, this all began when I opened those textbooks.

Was I willing to take such a risk? Perhaps I should stop and accept my role in the ministry. That would certainly involve less suffering than burning in hell for all eternity.

I did not know what to do. Not knowing what to think of next, I decided to think of nothing and accept my place before God. I was not to question him or his works. I was never to think that my own morality was greater than his. I determined I would never do so again. But, things change.

Shortly afterward, a young man who was 20 years old and who had been raised in the church where I ministered came out and informed everyone that he was gay. His friends at church were devastated. His best friend was in terrible shock, and she did not know how to handle this supposedly awful news.

After revealing this about himself, he did not return to church again. He stayed away. Church members declared he would not return because he felt so ashamed in his sin. I considered that I would not want to return to a group of people who had shown such rejection toward me. It felt inappropriate to decide how he was feeling when he was not even there to answer or explain himself.

As I watched this unfold, the questions returned with a vengeance. They were far too powerful for me to push away. This was impacting someone who was right in front of me… or at least he had been until rejection had driven him away. I pondered again the implications about God that this revealed.

This young man had not asked to be gay. He was simply born gay. All he had done was tell his friends about the way he was born. He had then suffered shock, appall, and rejection. Of course, no one told him not to attend church any longer. But, that does not constitute acceptance.

They did not accept that he was gay. Therefore, they did not accept him. Deep down, I knew that was true. It caused my heart to ache.

As difficult as this was to cope with, this very issue was soon going to strike much closer to my heart as I reunited with someone from my past. Its impact was going to deepen all the more.

HITTING CLOSE TO HOME

As all of these questions swirled around in my thoughts, I fought to push them away. I was unsuccessful in my efforts. If I accepted the answers that appeared to be true, I felt as though my entire life would dissolve. I wanted to know, and yet, I didn't.

I wanted the truth. But, I also wanted the truth to be what I wanted it to be. I wanted the personal, intimate, almighty God that I had come to know and love to be real and present with me each day. I wanted the years of my life I had lived thus far to mean what I had thought they had meant. I wanted it to be that those powerful moments I had experienced in so many church services and during my private prayer times were truly me entering the divine presence of God.

I wanted it all to be real, and I had no idea how I could continue in a world where none of those experiences were rooted in reality. I did not want to live in a world where I would never have such experiences ever again. Without God, I did not even know who I was. Giving up my faith would truly mean giving up my own self.

I did not know how to grasp such an idea on an any level. My experiences, my perception of the world, and my understanding of myself would all be gone if I were to abandon my faith. I had initially believed that I was going to sort all of this out and things would turn out alright. Now, I felt unsure whether that was true as my questions had only intensified rather than fading away.

It appeared that my faith was hurting people. I could not reconcile that realization.

Right then, out of the blue, I was contacted by someone with whom I had not spoken for the past few years. It was my ex-fiance. We had communicated here and there after I finished Bible College, but we had lost touch when I had moved.

I was no longer in love with him, but I did still love him as a friend very much. Even though we had lost contact, our bond of friendship was still deeply important to me. However, the little time we had spent together after the ending of our relationship was quite awkward as we attempted to delicately tread through the reality that he was no longer serving the Lord, I was, and I believed he was living the wrong kind of life.

Because of this, he did not seek me out often, and when I had moved away, he had decided to let me go. But, as both he and I had thought of one another through our bond of friendship, he changed his mind and decided to reach out. I was both shocked and thrilled to hear from him.

We chatted for hours, staying up literally most of the night talking about all we had been doing since we had last spoke. The phone call was over five hours long. The following night, we spoke for over four hours, staying up late once again.

We continued with phone conversations every few days over the following two weeks or so. We often laughed so hard, tears were streaming down my face. Once, I was laughing so hard, I began to choke, which only made both of us laugh all the more. I was so happy to have him back in my life.

Then, he decided it was time to come clean with me about something he felt he could no longer hide from me. During the phone calls, we had had multiple conversations of honesty that were so transparent and open, they were, at times, excruciating.

We were making peace with another and enjoying our

friendship once again. He realized under these circumstances, it would be morally wrong for him to withhold what he was about to tell me. He felt I deserved to know the truth. He revealed that he was gay.

I felt like the room was spinning. This could not be true. He explained that he was somewhat bisexual, so he did have some interest in women, but, for the most part, he was attracted to men, and he could not imagine going the rest of his life without any intimate or romantic involvement with another man.

He explained that he had indeed been in love with me during our relationship, but that was not even my concern at the time. We had both moved on from our relationship. Now, he was a friend that I cared about very deeply.

He told me that he was a homosexual, he had engaged in and still engages in homosexual activity, and he had no intention of stopping. My memory of the youth group bonfire burst into my thoughts.

If all I had been taught at church was true, he was going to burn in hell for all eternity. That was already more than I could take in. I then considered that if all that I had learned in my classes at school was true, God was the one who had made him this way to begin with.

It is one thing to imagine a theoretical person in a situation like this. It is entirely different when the person is real and is someone you know very well and have cared about for years.

Sadly, I followed the typical, evangelical Christian lines like the good, but struggling, Christian I was. I talked to him about God's plan for his life. I told him homosexuality was never in God's plan for people. The conversation immediately shut down.

We had spent hours upon hours talking on the phone until this point. Now, there was nothing to say. We ended the phone conversation and did not speak again after that. He stopped calling me and would not answer my phone calls to him.

I was very sad. I thought my dear friend was back in my life, but now, he was gone again. I hadn't judged him because he was hurting people. I had judged him because of his sexual orientation. While I did not want to fully admit it to myself, deep down, I recognized that our latest parting was entirely my fault.

THE SPROUTING SEEDS

My world had been turned upside down. I could reconcile absolutely nothing. I had a desire to serve God and a doubt as to whether anything I had ever believed was even true.

I began to think about the doubts I had briefly entertained in the past to which I had never given much thought. I recalled coming home to my parents and sharing with them that I did not believe that our founding fathers had been godly men like I had been told.

All those years later, I could still remember the images that had been displayed in my fifth grade history book. I was so immensely heartbroken and horrified to see people being treated in such ways. As a child, I could not understand how they had been treated like mere property and nothing more. Now, as an adult, I still did not understand how such atrocities could have happened in our country.

I wondered if it was true that our nation was intended to be a Christian nation dedicated to God. When I had wondered as a child, I did not have easy access to information that existed outside of our faith. But, now, I did. I had the internet. I also had access to a university library and had learned a basic understanding of how to use it.

I began to do some investigating. I discovered that my

doubts had some merit. Not all of our founding fathers were even professed Christians, let alone practicing, evangelical Christians. Thomas Jefferson and Benjamin Franklin, for example, definitely did not hold a religious view that was even remotely comparable to evangelical Christianity.

I considered that God is not mentioned in the constitution a single time. If this was truly intended to be a Christian nation, dedicated to God, with a government and laws founded entirely on the Bible, why was neither God nor the Bible mentioned a single time in the constitution?

Whether the founding fathers were Christian or otherwise said nothing about my faith itself. What mattered to me was how many times I had heard about our Christian foundation as a nation from the pulpit, in Sunday School, and in youth group. I had been repeatedly given wrong information.

Just as I had observed that I had received an incorrect presentation of the field of science by those I had turned to for the truth, I could see that they had been wrong about this, too. Knowing this, I began listening with skepticism to my senior pastor as he preached from the pulpit each Sunday, and I wondered if he had any idea what he was even talking about.

I considered the many times I myself had stood behind that same pulpit. Had I had any idea what I was talking about? How many times had I stood up there and said something, believing it to be true only because it had been repeatedly said to me over the years?

I thought about my questions and concerns about speaking in tongues that I had experienced as a teenager. I thought about the stories in the Bible and how they sometimes sounded silly to me. At night, I lay awake, wondering what it all meant. The world felt dark, cold, and unfamiliar. Nothing made sense.

I thought more about my ex-fiance. Was he truly deserving of being tortured forever and ever without end? God suddenly seemed less good and less righteous. Nothing about this sounded moral or just.

In spite of all of the questions and doubts that now flooded my mind, I still believed that, most likely, I would sort through all of this and reconcile with my faith eventually. The idea of living without my faith was simply too incomprehensible for me to grasp back then. The idea of my faith being completely wrong was even more unfathomable.

There was only one thing of which I had become absolutely certain. I was done with the ministry. I did not want to do this anymore. I did not feel I even could. I was not happy. I wanted to go to school full time.

Even though these questions were causing me turmoil, my studies themselves were enthralling to me. I loved doing my schoolwork. I felt happy and fulfilled. I wanted to do it more without distraction by the stresses of life in the ministry.

In spite of my difficulties and frustrations in the ministry, it was a heartbreaking decision. While the ministry did not seem to be my place, I did love the people and families I had come to know. I cherished them. I had friends that meant the world to me. I did not want to leave them.

However, I knew I had to do so. I wanted to study neuroscience and psychology, but there were not any options in that geographical area for that topic of study. I knew I would have to move somewhere else. I looked over the different universities around the country that offered the type of program I was looking for.

I hoped that my shallow and limited knowledge of the subject was the reason I could not fit what I had learned into my faith. Perhaps as I learned more, I would better understand how to make it all work.

I discovered a Jesuit university that offered grants and scholarships that I could qualify for in spite of already having a degree, and it had the type of program I was looking for. I was elated. This solved an enormous problem for me. Maybe there was a way to do this after all.

I was also relieved to have found a religiously-based university. While Catholicism and evangelical Christianity have plenty of differences between them, they at least believed in the Bible. I felt this university would offer me a safe space to explore my many questions. This university could provide multiple solutions to multiple problems in my life.

I applied and held my breath as I awaited their answer. Weeks passed. I wondered what I would do if I was not accepted. Taking out school loans for an entire 4-year degree was an overwhelming idea. I also did not want to attend a secular university given my struggles with my faith. I did not know what to do but hope.

Then, I finally received the letter in the mail. I had been accepted. Shortly afterward, I saw that I could receive enough grant funding to cover much of my first year there, only requiring me to borrow a relatively small amount. My decision was made.

I stood before the congregation, shaking and fighting tears. I looked out into the eyes of these people who I loved so much. In spite of my difficulties with ministry, I had many wonderful memories with them. I wished I did not have to leave them.

I announced that I was resigning. I heard audible gasps of surprise and shock from the congregation. My voice quivered as I explained why I had to leave. When I finished my announcement, they began to clap and I began to cry.

My stomach hurt. I felt like I might vomit. It was hard to

believe I was closing the chapter of ministry in my life, at least for now. But, I knew it was the right decision. I was going to go to this university, explore all there was to learn, and figure out what my future would now hold.

DEEPENING KNOWLEDGE

I had moved half way across the country again. I was overwhelmed with terror and excitement all at once. While I greatly missed my friends, I was relieved to no longer be in the ministry.

I set up my new, tiny apartment. I found my way to a local store to purchase cleaning supplies and basic necessities. I picked which cupboard would hold my plates and cups. I put my silverware in the drawer I deemed most suitable. I spread my comforter onto my bed.

My belongings and my small dog were the only piece of familiarity in my life. I was in a new city where I knew absolutely no one. I was alone.

Soon, I arrived on the campus of my new school. I was completely lost. This campus was enormous compared to the small Bible college I had attended, taking up several city blocks. I wandered around in confusion for quite some time until I finally found my first classroom.

I sat in the front row, eager to hear the first lecture. I had enrolled in a class called Genetics and Evolution that was an elective course for students pursuing majors outside of the sciences. I did not need to take this course to graduate as science electives were not required for those studying in the neuroscience program.

I decided to take this class anyway. I had so many questions, and I needed direct answers. Was it possible evolutionary theory was correct? Was evolution a baseless theory without supporting evidence like I had been told? I needed to know.

It seemed this class would provide the answer to these questions. If it was indeed a ridiculous and baseless theory, my faith would be affirmed. My doubts would be put to rest, and I could continue on as I had been.

If evolutionary theory did have some evidence supporting it...well, I did not know what would happen next. I only understood that I needed to know one way or the other.

The information I learned in this class changed my life. It did not change it in an instant, no. But, it ignited movement of the wheel of change, and that wheel would not stop turning even in spite of my efforts to hold it still.

When you learn information that, with certainty, contradicts your faith, you only have two options. You can either leave the religion and continue life with your new understanding, or you can stay in your religion and fake it as you continue life with your new understanding.

You cannot un-learn information. You cannot believe claims that you know are false. You cannot go in reverse. Life moves forward. Your only two options are to travel with it or to live a lie. This was the position I found myself in as I was presented with clear information that contradicted what I had believed thus far. The following is a summary of what I learned.

THE BASICS OF EVOLUTION

Before my professor began to introduce this information, he explained that it is important to define terms. We were going to be talking about species, populations, and individuals, and we should not move forward until we clearly established what each of these words means.

The word species, for the sake of discussion here, refers to a group of living organisms with similar traits who can produce viable offspring, meaning offspring that has the potential to survive and reproduce. While this may seem obvious, it is important to define these terms clearly.

Consider the horse and the donkey. Most would understand that these are two different species. However, a horse and a donkey can come together, turn on the love music, mate, and produce offspring. The result is a mule.

Mules are sterile, though. They cannot reproduce. So, while horses and donkeys can mate and produce offspring, they cannot produce *viable* offspring. Therefore, horses and donkeys are not the same species.

I followed along in the class so far just fine. "Alright, we are just talking about species and the fact that different species cannot successfully reproduce together. Sure, I can agree with that."

Within a species are populations. A population is a group of individuals of the same species living in the same geographical area. Field mice can be found in Illinois, but they can also be found in Nigeria. They are the same species, but different populations.

I considered that according to the Bible, two mice had been housed safely on the ark. Then, they had slowly repopulated the earth. That sounded good. I was ready for more.

Within populations are individual organisms, meaning, of

course, one living organism. It all sounded simple enough. I could handle this.

All populations of every species have variation. This means the individuals within that population are not all exactly the same. "Um, what?"

This surprised me. I had thought of the different individuals within a species as all being more or less the same with the exception of humans. As Christians, we considered ourselves to be special and separate from the natural world.

While we saw each human as a unique individual, we assumed tigers are tigers, warthogs are warthogs, and they are all the same. Now, this professor was explaining this was untrue.

I considered that my own experience with domesticated pets showed there is variation within a species. Even within the same breed of dogs, there is variation. My pet chihuahua was not exactly the same as my neighbor's pet chihuahua. They had many similarities (both barked tremendously more than their human companions desire). But, they had differences, too.

I realized this guy was right. All tigers are not the same. All warthogs are not the same. There are variations within every species and population.

The reason for this variation, he explained, is genetic mutation. When DNA copies itself, occasionally, an error is made. When it is, a genetic mutation occurs.

If that genetic mutation occurs within a sperm or egg, the mutation will be present in the individual formed from that sperm or egg. Sometimes, the mutation causes a trait in the individual that is catastrophic, and the individual cannot survive or reproduce. This is the most common result of a genetic mutation.

Other times, the mutation causes a trait that is entirely benign and has no impact on the organism in any way. Other times, the mutation results in a trait that is advantageous for the organism.

I had previously learned that God was the reason each of us was unique. I considered that if variation existed amongst animals as well, and genetic mutations were the reason, I at first assumed God was the one causing the mutations. That was simply the means through which he created these individuals exactly the way they were supposed to be.

However, as I listened to examples of genetic mutations we have observed in nature, I realized if God were behind these mutations, he would have to be incredibly cruel. Often, genetic mutations lead to severe deformities that cause the animal to suffer greatly until death. What reason would God have for doing something so egregious?

In Sunday School, the blame would have been placed on the sin of Adam and Eve. But, a baby giraffe being born without legs had nothing to do with the act chosen by a couple of humans thousands of years before. Why should that giraffe suffer over something like this? It made no sense.

My professor offered a different answer. He explained in great detail exactly how various genetic mutations happen. They were random and without cause. Sometimes, they had painful consequences, but that is what happens when a process is random. A random, meaningless process made much more sense for something like this.

I wanted to believe otherwise. I wanted to believe God was behind all of this. However, the more I learned, the more I saw not only that God was not necessary for these processes to occur, but that if God were indeed a part of them, he would have to be heartless and even vicious.

I would love to get into more detail about genetic mutations and how those mutations translate into traits here. There is so much more we could delve into. However, I am writing this book with the beginner in mind.

If you would like to learn about this subject in more detail, I have included additional information in the appendix, which you can flip to now or when you get to the end of the book. Of course, there is much more to learn even beyond what I have included in the appendix, but going deeper is beyond the scope of this book.

If you are curious, and I hope you are, please look over the recommended reading listed in the appendix to learn how and where to further explore this topic. For our purposes here, suffice it to say that populations have variation because of genetic mutations. New or altered genes make their way into populations through this means.

Some traits within these populations are advantageous, making it more likely that an individual with them will survive and/or reproduce. Other traits are less advantageous, and those born with them will struggle more to survive and reproduce.

Those individuals with the more advantageous traits survive and/or reproduce and pass on their genes at a higher rate than those that do not have those traits. This does not in any way mean that one individual with a specific trait survives while all others immediately die. That is not how it works.

Rather, the individuals with an advantageous trait produce offspring at a higher rate (thereby passing on that trait to the next generation at a higher rate) than those without the advantageous trait. Over the course of many generations, that trait will then show up more and more often in a population until eventually, nearly all members of that population have that particular trait.

In this way, through natural selection, populations adapt to their environment more and more as time passes, and the individuals in that population become more "fit" for their particular environment.

I came to understand that my perception of the world had been backward. Mountain goats were so perfectly suited to their environment that it appeared God had made that environment just for them. We humans require a specific atmosphere to breathe, and so, I believed God had created the atmosphere just right so we and other species could breathe.

Everything I was learning suggested the reverse. The environment existed first, and we adapted to it. The atmosphere was not made to match our lungs. Our lungs evolved to fit with the atmosphere.

The thought was jarring. It completely and utterly destroyed the idea of God designing a world with us in mind. Surely, this could not be true. I pondered the claim I had so often heard that we could not have possibly come to be through this process. There was too much involved in the formation of a new species. It could not happen without God. Or could it?

MICRO-EVOLUTION VS MACRO-EVOLUTION

Among creationist circles, there is often a discussion about micro-evolution versus macro-evolution. They often identify and accept micro-evolution, explaining this simply means that species change a little bit over time, but they deny macro-evolution, the idea that entirely new species can form over time.

Antelope may slowly become able to run a little faster and a little faster over successive generations. Monkeys may become a little more adept at climbing trees over time. But, antelope always remain antelope, and monkeys always remain monkeys. That is what creationists claim, and that is what I believed as I sat in the desk in my classroom.

Macro-evolution, the beginning of a new species, never

happens, according to the creationist. I quickly learned, though, that evolutionary biologists would not agree in the slightest.

So, how do new species form? Is it really possible to begin with a bacteria and end up with a human being? The thought sounded absurd to me.

My professor stood before us and explained that the formation of a new species happens through environmental change. Environmental change, for a species, can happen in one of two ways. The first way is through a population breaking apart and a portion of that population moving to a different location.

For example, imagine a population living on an island together. It is a population of bogwacks (yes, that is a made up, fictional species). One year, the water level drops unusually low, creating temporary passage to a different, nearby island. Some bogwacks wander over that passage to the different island.

The water level rises again to its normal level, and so, those bogwacks that crossed over cannot return to the original island and rejoin their original population. They have therefore now established a new population of bogwacks on the new island.

The new island is not the same as the previous island. Therefore, the traits that are advantageous on the first island may not necessarily be advantageous on the second.

Similarly, imagine a group of goopubs (yes, another made up, fictional species) living on one side of a mountain. Occasionally, a couple of adventurous goopubs wander over to the other side of the mountain. The environments on either side of a mountain range tend to be quite different from one another, and the more steep a mountain range is, the greater the difference.

When air approaches a mountain range, it cannot pass

through the mountain. It has to go over it. As the air moves upward on its way over the mountain, it cools and thins. This causes it to drop the moisture it was carrying in the form of rain.

By the time it reaches the top and crosses over, the air will have lost most or all its moisture. Thus, one side of the mountain will be green and lush with life as it receives lots of rain. Conversely, the other side of the mountain will be dry and largely barren as it receives very little rain.

The traits that help an individual survive in a desert will differ from the traits that help an individual survive in a lush forest. We can see from this that whether by moving to a different island, crossing a mountain range, or another type of move, the individuals that go somewhere else will end up in a different environment with different selection pressures.

The selection pressures in a desert for a particular species, for example, may be to be smaller so the individual requires less food and water to survive. However, upon moving to an environment with more ample food and water, being small no longer provides that particular advantage.

In the new environment, perhaps being bigger provides an advantage. In addition, in the desert, individuals will blend in with the environment better (and therefore, be less likely to be seen by a predator) if they are similarly colored as rocks or dirt. In a more lush environment, it would be more advantageous to be similarly colored as grass and leaves. This is what I mean by differing selection pressures in different environments.

Notice the selection pressures are not always to become bigger, stronger, and smarter. Many people misunderstand evolution and believe the strongest are the ones to survive. The reality is that the most fit survive and reproduce at a higher rate, and what is fit for a particular group of organisms depends on the environment in which they live.

THE FORMATION OF NEW SPECIES

Let us return to our scenario in which some bogwacks moved to a different island and created a new population. Over a very large number of generations, the bogwacks on that island will develop more and more traits that are different from the traits of the bogwacks on the first island because they are living in areas with different selection pressures.

Over many more generations, these changes can become so numerous and vast that if a bogwack from the second island came across an individual from the first island, they would not be able to reproduce viable offspring together. When this happens, the bogwacks on the second island are no longer actually bogwacks. They have become a different species. They are now wompazees.

Suppose years later, some wompazees then move to yet a third island, creating a second population of wompazees. That population will change all the more over many generations. Now, you can end up with individuals that are even more different from the bogwacks still living on the original island. This process is called adaptive radiation.

Another way that a population can end up in a new environment is not through travel to a new area, but due to climate changes or other environmental changes where the population resides. Such changes could include the introduction of a new species or the elimination of a specific food source.

The change in environment then creates new selection pressures. Over many, many generations, the individuals in that population will either not survive and the population will vanish, which happens in many cases, or they will change more and more as generations pass until they are quite different from their "mother" population.

Should they come across an individual from a different population that did not experience the same environmental changes, they may be so different that they can no longer mate and reproduce viable offspring. The population living in the area that underwent environmental change is now a new species.

Imagine this process happening again and again over millions upon millions of years and more. How much change could happen over that amount of time? Now, imagine how much change could happen over the course of three billion years.

Picture what would happen if I built a model house out of Legos®, and every once in a while, I walked by and moved one of the Legos® ever so slightly. Perhaps I detach one Lego® and snap it back on facing a different direction. The next time, I detach a Lego® and reattach it in a different location entirely. The next time, I add a Lego® that was not there before.

You would not notice much, if anything, after a few changes like this or even after 10-20. If I did so four million times, however, the resulting structure would be dramatically different than it was in the beginning. Maybe it would not even be a house any longer. Maybe it would be a car or a bridge.

You can see through this analogy that accepting the reality of what creationists call micro-evolution necessitates the acceptance of macro-evolution. You cannot have one without the other. Small changes accumulate to create large differences over time.

There are many other concepts and principles relevant to this discussion, such as sexual selection, gene flow, genetic drift, and many more. These principles and concepts are beyond the scope of this book. We have only scratched the surface of the surface here.

However, if your interest has been sparked and you desire to learn more, you will find more information in the appendix. If your thirst for this knowledge continues from there, please see the recommended books listed in the appendix as well. There is a wealth of fascinating information out there waiting for you to discover, and I strongly encourage you to read and learn more about the world in which you live.

I took all of this in. I began to see that yes, we can indeed begin with a bacteria or an even more primitive cell and, given enough time, eventually, end up with a human being through the process of evolution.

I did not know whether this theory was correct as I had not yet learned the evidence for it. However, I did understand that it was untrue that it did not make sense. Evolutionary theory actually made a lot of sense. It involved a length of time that is difficult for our minds to grasp simply because our lives are so comparatively short. But, it all seemed possible.

I was numb. Still, I determined I was going to continue to learn about what was out there. I had signed up for this class to hear it out, and I was going to do that.

THE EVIDENCE

Of course, it is one thing to say something is true and another thing entirely to provide the evidence for it. In science, doing the former alone is never acceptable. I understood this.

I learned that we have observed the result of adaptive radiation in nature. A great place to look is the Galapagos islands. For example, there are land iguanas that live in an area in the Galapagos islands where cacti and leaves are available. They have therefore adapted to receive nourishment and hydration from these sources.

Marine iguanas, on the other hand, live on shores of cooled, hardened lava, away from the snakes living more inland who would secure their doom. These iguanas have traits that allow them to swim to the bottom of the sea, eat seaweed, and then, return to the shore.

As much as this information was causing me genuine pain as it conflicted with my faith so greatly, I was elated to learn there were iguanas that swam in the sea. Prior to this, I had had no idea that such creatures existed. I had set aside my curiosity of and fascination with the different species living in the world for so many years. Now, I was connecting with it once again, and that aspect of this journey felt wonderful.

When Darwin visited the Galapagos Islands, he studied the finches living on each of the islands. Some of them were ground finches who used heavy beaks to crush seeds. On other islands, they ate the flowers of cacti and had beaks suitable for doing so. On yet other islands were tree finches, and most of those ate insects.

The woodpecker finch has a stout, straight beak that it uses to bore into wood in search of insects to eat. Once it has found one, amazingly, it uses a cactus spine or a twig to remove the insect and consume it.

The point here is that each population of finches is adapted to successfully receive nourishment from the specific food source available to them on their particular island. Interestingly, if we travel to South America and observe finches there on the mainland, we see no such diversity in their beaks. We only see this diversity on islands.

Some finches, at some point, made their way off the mainland and over to the Galapagos Islands. Those with beaks slightly more suitable to obtain the food source on the particular island they ended up on survived and reproduced at a higher rate than those that did not. Over the course of generations, their beaks slowly changed to adapt to the available food source there.

The peppered moth is a commonly used example regarding environmental change and a resulting change in traits amongst a population. The industrial revolution brought about pollution that had previously not been there. In forests with more pollution where the trees were a darker color, the peppered moths living there were mostly a darker color as well. In contrast, in less polluted areas with lighter colored trees, the moths are lighter colored.

This observation of peppered moths, made by a scientist named Bernard Kettlewell, drew some criticism in the 1990s as some scientists claimed he had falsified data. Creationists latched onto this claim with vigor and declared that evolutionary biologists were a fraud.

However, another scientist named Michael Majerus completed a seven-year experiment that tested Kettlewell's claims and their criticisms. His data was published in 2012, and it vindicated Kettlewell and his experiments. Indeed, the peppered moth was an example of natural selection at work that was easy to observe and understand, and indeed, evolutionary theory is testable.

The creationists then responded with silence. They had been so quick to shout what they perceived as evidence to support their view and when they learned that that evidence actually did not support their view, they simply ignored it.

I began to notice a pattern. The creationists were the ones who were standing up and declaring the truth, expecting others to believe their claims without any supporting evidence. Scientists, for every claim they presented to me, presented data along with it.

THE WHOLE PICTURE

Many creationists have suggested that these observations are not the result of organisms adapting to their environment over time, but are instead a sign of God's work. God created each species with his own hand and designed them to perfectly match the environment in which he put them.

I wanted that to be true. But, I had learned enough to know that it was not a correct proposition.

The environment changes. This earth has been through an ice age, for example, and that is only one of many examples I could choose. If organisms did not adapt in response to environmental change, there would be no living organisms on this planet.

I wondered, though, what are the odds that everything would go just right when this happened? Could that be the sign of God in all of this?

Unfortunately, the reality is that the majority of species that have ever existed on this earth are now extinct. We know this due to the fossil record, which we will discuss in more detail soon.

Not all populations manage to adapt. It goes wrong much more frequently than it goes right. When it goes wrong, the members of that population all eventually die as a result. Only those populations that were lucky enough to have amongst them the particular trait necessary to adapt after a change continued on. Most populations and species that have once lived on this earth were not so lucky.

Once again, it occurred to me that if God was behind all of this, it was a sign that he was utterly cruel and malicious. Either that or just incredibly irresponsible, inefficient, and/or incompetent.

If I were hired by a company to manufacture a product and demonstrated a failure rate of over 99.9%, I would be fired immediately. I would certainly not be promoted to the head of the company.

Imagine a massive earthquake striking a city in which one million people were residing. When it was over, all but ten people were killed in the catastrophe. Would the ten survivors be a sign that a supreme being was in control of everything? Or would it appear that just a handful got lucky and something extremely horrific had happened?

We would be foolish to suggest that circumstances going just right ten times out of a million is indicative of a supernatural force and a master plan while ignoring the 999,990 times that everything went completely wrong. It is important to take in the whole picture.

For most species that ever lived on this earth, circumstances went horribly wrong. What we see today in nature is only the comparatively small handful of survivors for whom things managed to go just right.

As I considered this, I reflected on a common argument I had made in the past to support the existence of God. I argued that the world appeared so organized, it were as though it had been intentionally put together. This may have been easy for me to say being born in a wealthy country with all of the privileges that automatically afforded to me.

I began to wonder if the child born into extreme poverty in a third world country would have agreed with me that the world appeared organized and intentionally designed as he breathed his last breath after slowly starving to death in agony. Likely not.

When we are only looking at the victorious survivors, the world can seem much more organized than it actually is. If we take the time to observe the extreme amount of pain, death, and extinction that has occurred on this planet, though, the idea of a design will be difficult to grasp. Can a design with a 99.9% failure rate be considered a design at all?

TESTING EVOLUTION IN NATURE

All that aside, I listened to my professor describe the results of adaptive radiation we can observe such as the finches being suited to their food sources on different islands. But, how do we know for sure this is the result of the process described? It seems to make sense, but making sense is not evidence.

Ken Ham, a prominent creationist, claims that evolutionary

biology is a special kind of science called "historical science." He claims that we cannot study it appropriately because we were not there when it happened, and since we cannot directly observe evolution occurring, it cannot be studied.

My professor then taught us that we have observed evolution occur with our own eyes. We have even reproduced it. A common creationist argument is that evolution is not scientific because it is not testable when in truth, it absolutely is testable and has been tested many, many times.

Ken Ham is wrong. He is wrong in about every way that a person can be wrong. But, I used to listen to people just like him because they told me what I wanted to hear. And the only reason I wanted to hear it is because it is what I had always heard.

There are certainly significant challenges with designing experimental studies in evolutionary biology. Adaptive changes in traits occur over many generations.

Think of the tortoise, which can live between 80 and 120 years. No human could possibly observe multiple generations of these species. In cases such as these, a study would have to run for well over a thousand years to adequately collect even a very basic amount of data. This is clearly not practical.

In other cases, however, adaptive changes occur more quickly. Species with shorter life spans (and thus, a more rapid generation turnover rate) provide opportunities for us to observe evolution in a single human lifetime.

One such example took place on two small islands off Croatia, Pod Kopiste and Pod Mrcaru. On Pod Kopiste, a species of lizard, *Podarcis sicula*, which ate primarily insects was observed. Its generation turnover is around two years, making it a much more suitable choice than a species of elephant or tortoise.

The neighboring island, Pod Mrcaru, had no such lizards

living on it, which offered an opportunity to run an experiment. In 1971, a group of scientists captured five pairs of these lizards from Pod Kopiste and released them onto Pod Mrcaru. Scientists returned in 2008 and looked to see if there were any lizards on Pod Mrcaru, and indeed, there were.

DNA testing confirmed these lizards were the species *Podcarcis sicula*. However, the lizards on Pod Mrcaru had notable differences from those living on Pod Kopiste.

On Pod Mrcaru, the heads of the lizards were larger than those on Pod Kopiste. Their heads were longer, wider, and taller. This change in head shape offered greater jaw strength to the lizards, which was more suitable for an organism consuming plants rather than insects. And indeed, these lizards on Pod Mrcaru were eating plants, not insects.

Small changes in the guts that are associated with a more herbivorous diet were also observed in the lizards on Pod Mrcaru. While these lizards had certainly not become a new species, the changes were clear and observable as the lizards had adapted (and will continue to adapt) to their new environment. If the environments on these two islands differ enough, the lizards on Pod Mrcaru may change to the point of becoming a different species given enough time (recall my example of the house built of Legos® earlier in this book).

While there are many places in the world like this in which we could create a "lab" to run an experiment, we have to be careful with doing so. Introduction of a new species into an environment through human intervention can lead to an unintended ecological disaster that can easily spiral out of our control.

On Christmas Island off the northwest shores of Australia, a famous march of the crabs happens annually as literally millions of crabs leave the forest of the island and migrate to the ocean to breed. It is an amazing spectacle.

Cargo boats inadvertently carried yellow crazy ants from Africa to this island. Having no natural predators on the island, the ants flourished and established an extremely large population there. The ants attack crabs by squirting acid into their eyes and blinding them. The blinded crabs are doomed.

The yellow crazy ants have killed or displaced up to 20 million crabs on Christmas Island. But, this has not only affected the crabs. The red crabs perform an important function in the forest as they dig and fertilize the soil and control the weeds. The structure of the forest has changed as the crab population has decreased so significantly, which has in turn impacted other species who depend on the forest for survival.

As you can see, we should not travel around the world, carelessly introducing species onto islands for the purpose of observing their resulting adaptation and evolution. We could inadvertently wreak havoc on the environment by doing so.

We need another way that is fully within our control in a lab. Fortunately, such a way exists. Since 1988, 12 lines of bacteria have been studied in a laboratory setting, and many evolutionary experiments have been conducted through this means. We have learned valuable information about DNA, genetic mutations, and adaptation through these brilliant experiments.

If you look in the appendix in "Testing Evolution in a Lab," you can find more detailed information about these experiments that have repeatedly tested evolutionary theory in a carefully controlled setting within a laboratory. Feel free to read through it now or when you reach the end of this book.

THE FOSSIL RECORD

There is far too much information to share from the fossil record than could be shared in a book like this. So, I will only touch on this here. However, there is a treasure trove of information about the fossil record and the amazing revelations it offers us about the history of our world. In the appendix, I have listed suggestions for additional reading so you can learn more, and I encourage you to do more digging on this subject, no pun intended.

I don't believe there is any greater example of the ignorance of evolutionary theory amongst evangelical Christians than the presentation of the crocoduck, presented by Kirk Cameron and Ray Comfort (both evangelical Christians and creationists). It is a picture of a fictitious animal with the head of a crocodile on the body of a duck.

Creationists use the crocoduck to laugh at evolutionary biologists, claiming that the theory of evolution requires such a creature exist. Of course, pictures of the crocoduck are then used by those who understand evolutionary theory to respond to creationists in kind.

I'm thankful I was not in the faith at the time the crocoduck gained its popularity amongst creationists because I am sure I would have seized it with fervor. However, I did once make ridiculous arguments, describing events such as a gorilla giving birth to a dog and so forth. My friends and I laughed and laughed. I thought evolutionary biologists were fools.

Now, after all I had learned already and all I was in the process of learning about the fossil record, I realized I was the one who had been the fool. I hadn't thought evolutionary theory was ridiculous because the evidence suggested it was. I thought it was ridiculous because I had not even looked at the evidence before deciding what to think of it.

Creationists use the crocoduck to claim that transitional fossils like these have never been found. Therefore, they conclude, evolutionary theory is false and without evidence and creationism is true. As they do so, they clearly demonstrate a belief that evolutionary theory claims that ducks are very close descendants of crocodiles or vice versa (they aren't).

While their presentation of the crocoduck is certainly fictional, there actually is a "crocoduck" of sorts that once existed. An ancient creature has been found in the fossil record that is like a crocodile in many ways, but its head has a bill similar to that of a duck. It stood more upright on its four legs rather than on the legs we see on crocodiles today, which stick more out of their sides.

More study into the fossil record revealed that ducks and crocodiles both descended from this creature. They are very distant cousins to one another. One did not descend from the other.

Transitional fossils like these exist and have been discovered in huge numbers. I will diverge for a moment here and mention that one could reasonably argue that all fossils are transitional fossils. Many seem to think that a transitional species existed specifically so it could serve as a stepping stone to the next species. But, this could not be further from the truth.

Those species we like to think of as transitional actually existed in that manner because those were the traits that best benefited the individuals at that time in that environment. Traits did not exist so that they could contribute to a more "advanced" trait down the road. They existed for their own reasons for the individual that lived right then.

Of course, in spite of this, seeing these intermediary stages in the fossil record greatly helps us explore the history of life on our planet. In fact, transitional fossils have provided a wonderful way to test hypotheses regarding specific components of evolutionary theory.

When a scientist hypothesizes the link between a genus of species, that scientist can predict, if the hypothesis is correct, the type of fossil that should be found in a specific geographical region that is a specific age. A team then begins to search for such a fossil. If the fossil is found, it contains the characteristics predicted, and it is of the right age, the hypothesis is confirmed. As you can see in this scenario, evolutionary theory is indeed testable.

Of course, the fossil record is incomplete, and we would expect it to be. The conditions required for a fossil to form rarely occur. There are many now extinct species who lived on this earth for whom we will never find fossilized remains. We will never know exactly what they looked like.

Still, fossils showing transitional stages in evolutionary history are far from rare. While the conditions for fossilization are uncommon, the fact is that the earth is billions of years old, so there were still lots of opportunities for fossilization to occur in spite of its rareness. Therefore, even though we do not have every single step of transitions between groupings of species, we have enough of the steps filled in in the fossil record that the fact that the transitions happened is undeniable to any reasonable person.

As I mentioned, there is so much more to learn about the fossil record that is beyond the scope of this book. If this information has sparked your interest, I have provided an additional section in the appendix all about fossils. If you are still left hungry for more information after reading that section, please look over the Additional Reading in the appendix and discover that which awaits your discovery.

Just as the last chapter was only scratching the surface of the surface of evolutionary theory, this compilation of brief summaries of the evidence for evolution is only scratching the surface of the surface of the evidence. Evolutionary theory is supported by an enormous amount of data that has been meticulously collected through carefully conducted scientific experiments.

As I read, listened, and learned throughout my first full-time semester at school, I firmly understood I had been duped. I had been told again and again that evolutionary theory was ridiculous and had no supporting evidence. That claim was wrong.

I did not wake up from there and abandon my faith, however. Leaving one's world in its entirety cannot happen that quickly. But, I had come to see that at least some of the information I had been told was incorrect. There was no doubt that that was true. I was not sure what that meant for me, my faith, or the world.

I only knew one thing: the creationist story from Genesis was not how we, or any life on earth, had come to be. Now, I had to figure out what to do with that information.

CREATIONISM

M y head was spinning. The first semester was over, and I felt as though I had been run over by a bull-dozer filled with knowledge and information. I don't want to misrepresent this experience. I absolutely loved my class, Genetics and Evolution, as well as my other classes.

Every single class lecture and page turn of my textbooks, I was enthralled by the information I had learned. As I walked the halls of the large building that contained most of my classes, I had never felt so alive.

I had managed to land a job working in an entry level position on a research team. My days were spent listening to class lectures, studying, and working in the lab. My evenings were filled with studying at home. My grades came in, and I had received all As. I realized I truly had an aptitude for learning this subject matter. I loved it.

That feeling of emptiness I had lived with for so long had completely vanished. Every single day, I was thrilled with what I was doing. I was fulfilled. I was where I belonged. I was where I had always belonged. I love science. I had always loved science.

All those years, that nagging, gnawing feeling was there because I was not following my own unique path. I had had my path defined for me long before I was old enough to make my own decisions. I had spent my life forcing myself into a circle when I was actually shaped like a trapezoid. Now, I was where I fit. This had become clear to me.

FAITH AND DOUBT

As happy as I was with my daily life, I was living with internal torment. I still loved God. I still wanted to please God. But, I was not even sure how I could reconcile my faith with everything I had learned.

I firmly understood that evolutionary theory was absolutely not a baseless and ridiculous theory like I had been told. It was supported by a mountain of data. It was not ridiculous; it was perfectly rational. There was absolutely no chance that the creation story in Genesis was true. Human beings are here because of evolution. This I knew for sure.

But, I also had my faith. I wanted to have both of these, but they were mutually exclusive. My religion stated that the Bible was the inerrant word of God. It was true, word for word. The stories were not to be taken as allegory or symbolic. Fundamentalist Christianity demanded one interpret the Bible as literal truth from start to finish, including creationism. Now, I knew that I could not meet that demand.

Creationism, if you did not know, refers to the belief that the Genesis account of creation is scientifically accurate. There are young earth creationists and old earth creationists. Young earth creationists believe that less than 10,000 years ago, God created the earth and, in the span of one week, created all of the diversity of life that we see on earth today.

Old earth creationists believe that God created the earth millions or billions of years ago. They also believe that the "seven days" referred to in the Bible do not each represent one literal day, but simply an era of time. In one era, he created the land animals. In another era, he created the stars. And so forth.

Genesis lists the order of events of creation. The earth, it says, was created first. Then, God created light (the sun and the moon). The Bible refers to the moon as a source of light (we now know that the moon actually reflects the light of the sun and does not produce any light). After that, God created the stars.

Neither interpretation of this chapter could be true. If all of the stars were younger than the earth, we would not be able to see many of them. When you look up into the night sky and observe the stars, you are not observing many of those stars as they currently are. You are observing them as they once were.

They are so far away from us that by the time their light waves reach our eyes, millions or billions of years have passed since those light waves first left the star from whence they came. You can look into the night sky this evening and see stars that no longer even exist because so much has changed since those light waves left the star that once was.

The universe is very old, much older than the earth. The earth is comparatively young compared to the age of many of the stars that exist or once existed in the cosmos. The earth did not appear first. Virtually nothing about the creation story is possible, not even the order of events.

A question entered my mind, and I was finally in a place in which I could truly give this question actual thought. What if my religion was not true?

My chest turned cold. My arms began to feel numb. The very idea was shocking. I recalled the many times I had spoken with God during hours of personal darkness. What if all of those times, no one was actually listening? What if I was only talking to the air?

To put this in perspective, I'm sure most of us have gone through the terrible experience of losing a friend, whether through the severing of a friendship or through death. It is terrible and tragic. It is shocking, and we grieve.

With that in mind, imagine what it would feel like to learn your friend had never even existed. How would you feel to learn that all of your memories with that friend were simply a figment of your imagination? I was facing not only the loss of the future with my friend, but the past as well.

The thought that I might be out here in the world alone without a supernatural being looking out for me was terrifying. How could I explain the tragedies I had experienced in a way that gave me any sense of peace at all?

I thought of friends I had lost over the years. I had lost two friends in terrible car accidents and another dear friend to cancer. The only feeling of peace I had found was the belief that I would see them again someday. What if I wouldn't? Could I cope with that?

As I contemplated the implications of my religion having been wrong, some old seeds deep in my memories began to sprout all the more. How many sermons had I sat through as the preacher shouted about the religious beginnings of our country?

This nation was founded on the Bible and intended to be a nation that serves God, they would say. All of the laws and cultural practices were to be based solely on evangelical Christianity. But, those godless liberals had come along and pulled this country down, corrupting it and turning it toward the devil.

I remembered my fifth grade history class. I could still picture the images from my book of African American men, women, and children standing on platforms as slave owners bid to purchase them.

I could see the scars on their backs from their horrific journey across the sea during which no care was given to their very lives, let alone their comfort. They were seen as property, not people. I imagined what it must have been like for those people. I could not fathom that a single one of them would have agreed that our country back then was a godly, moral nation.

I thought about the many people I had heard speak in tongues. I truly, for the first time, took the time to think more deeply about it. I remembered my own experience being baptized in the Holy Spirit.

While speaking in tongues seemed to flow so naturally once it began, I was the one who first spoke those sounds. Maybe it is something any of us could do if we tried. Why did each individual seem to sound the same each time he/she spoke in tongues? Maybe it was not real.

I then thought about the stories of the Old Testament. So many of them did sound pretty odd. Could I really believe a man was swallowed by a whale for three days and lived to tell the tale?

As I learned more about the different species around the world, I had come to understand that two of every species could not possibly have fit onto Noah's ark. Even if they could, how did they get from the mountain on which the ark rested back to their original homes?

How did kangaroos get to Australia from there, and even if they did, why were all of them in Australia? Why don't we see populations of kangaroos between the mountain on which the ark rested and Australia, showing the path they took from the ark?

A feeling of panic rushed through me. I prayed that God would give me faith. I recalled the Scripture in which Jesus says that faith the size of a mustard seed is strong enough to move mountains. My faith had weakened for sure, but could my tiny grain of faith that remained get me through this?

I had no idea who to talk to. Asking these kinds of questions was not a welcomed practice in evangelical Christianity. I had seen it happen before. Sure, my fellow Christians would claim it is ok to ask questions and work through doubts. But, when those questions were actually asked, the response was anger and isolation.

Another thought occurred to me. Would I not only lose God through all of this, but my earthly friends, too? If I decided to leave my religion, would my friendships survive? I did not have any other friends. Would I end up all alone?

I knew I had to reach out to someone. I finally sat down with a minister and his wife who were dear friends of mine and who I trusted completely. I asked my questions, and I asked for help.

They cared. They really did. They were kind and gentle throughout the entire conversation. But, their answers came up short. They could not answer any of my questions. It was clear they had not thought deeply about these issues just as I had not done for so many years.

They wanted to answer my questions so they could help me. But, they just could not. Still, it felt very good to tell someone that this was happening and to still be accepted and loved. I was greatly relieved. Maybe I could get through this after all.

They encouraged me to trust God's word over man's. Man's understanding is limited, but God knows everything. He is so far above us, it is not our place to question his word. This is why faith is so important.

They then referred me to an organization called Reasons to Believe. I began to read opinion pieces from various creationists who claimed that the study of the earth revealed that the creation story was entirely factual while proving evolutionary theory wrong.

I considered that in school that semester, I had only heard one side of the story. Perhaps there was more that would bring clarity and help me figure this out without losing my faith.

I researched several creationists, not only those found through Reasons to Believe. To my disappointment, the arguments they offered did not provide the solid answers I had hoped for.

"SOMETIMES, SCIENTISTS ARE WRONG"

Some creationists point out times in which science had gotten something wrong. To them, this means evolutionary theory could not be trusted because science changes and what is currently believed is not always correct.

They are indeed correct that the understanding of science can sometimes change. After all, humans used to think the earth was flat and the sun revolved around the earth.

A small number of doctors used to believe that lobotomies were an appropriate treatment for mental illness, and many people were severely and irreversibly damaged because of this. The periodic table of elements is not exactly the same today as it was when it was first accepted. As more information has been learned, it has been updated to reflect that new information.

I read creationists claiming that because science has not always been correct, none of it can be trusted to any degree, and they agreed with this fully. However, I could not swallow this argument.

The fact that science changes in response to newly discovered information is one of its strengths, not its weakness. There is a humility in accepting that we do not know everything and that the understanding of the world that we currently hold could potentially change upon new discoveries.

This is in stark contrast to the evangelical view, which is to accept and embrace one set of information as 100% correct without ever questionings its truthfulness ever again. At least in science, if we get something wrong, there is always the possibility that it will be corrected down the road. But, with faith, if we get something wrong, we will always be wrong. There is no hope of correction.

Further, since the development of modern science, there has never been a discovery so revolutionary that it completely eliminated a scientific theory that had been supported by large amounts of data from multiple fields of science. When science gets something wrong, it is typically one particular aspect of a theory that we then improve upon or alter. We don't simply erase an entire theory and begin from scratch all over again when this happens (though scientists would do so if proper evidence was provided to call for such a change).

Evolutionary theory is supported by a large amount of data that has been tested and confirmed again and again and again throughout multiple fields of science. Small components of it are improved upon to accommodate new discoveries, but the basis of the theory has been confirmed so many times in so many different ways by so many different people working in so many different fields, the chances of it ever being disregarded as a whole are nearly zero.

Why say nearly zero instead of zero? Because a good scientist is always open to changing his/her mind upon the presentation of new data. If someone were to prove evolutionary theory wrong and offer another theory, scientists would embrace it if that person had the necessary data to support his/her claims.

For now, the creationist must decide whether he/she will go with a theory that has a .0000000000000000000000001% chance of being wrong or an idea that has an even smaller number than that percentage chance of being right.

The self-correcting nature of science is a component that should increase our trust in the scientific process. It is not a weakness. It is a strength. I did not find satisfaction in this claim. Instead, I was greatly bothered by it.

"SCIENTISTS DISAGREE ABOUT SOME COMPONENTS"

I read creationists claim that scientists do not agree about all components of evolutionary theory. That is absolutely correct. There is plenty of debate and discussion as we slowly form our evolutionary tree.

This argument is used by creationists to claim that evolutionary theory is questionable. To me, this explanation seemed to be a bit ironic coming from a Christian. Christianity has literally thousands of denominations and sects because they don't agree on so many components of the faith.

Will the rapture occur before the tribulation, half way through the tribulation, or after the tribulation? Will there be a rapture at all? Ask these two questions to lots of different Christians from lots of different denominations, and you will get lots of different answers.

Is there such a thing as the baptism in the Holy Spirit? Does the Holy Spirit enable a person to speak in tongues? There is no agreement whatsoever among Christians as to the answers to these questions.

They don't even agree about issues relevant to salvation, the most core component of Christianity. Once a person has received salvation, can he/she lose it? Is salvation available to anyone or does God select specific people to become saved, revealing himself only to those people? Christians cannot even agree on these core issues.

If the fact that there is disagreement on the details means that an entire idea should be thrown out through the window, then all Christians should renounce their faith immediately. Has any other religion in the history of mankind been more divided and fractured than Christianity?

Evolutionary theory has a vast amount of evidence supporting it. Nothing in biological science can be understood without a basic understanding of evolution. The fact that there is disagreement about some of the minor details does not discount the vast amount of evidence for the theory as a whole.

As scientists learn more, they refine and improve their understanding and move toward full agreement. Can Christians say the same?

This is the excitement and wonder of science. The fact that we do not know everything means there is more to discover. To me, that is a wonderful thought.

"IF THERE IS NO GOD, HOW DOES X HAPPEN?"

This is the classic "God of the gaps" argument. I witnessed creationists use it frequently. The claim is that if we don't understand how a component of nature works, that must mean God does it. This has been the default thinking throughout humanity.

When humans did not understand why or how it rained, they attributed storms to Zeus. But, as the gaps in our knowledge have been filled in more and more over time, God has been disappearing more and more from nature as a result.

How arrogant must we be to assume that we have the

capacity to understand virtually every naturally occurring event in the universe? How conceited to propose that we have found all of the evidence that could possibly be attained. That is the implication of these claims.

There are aspects of this universe that are beyond our ability to comprehend. That does not mean they are not entirely natural. Our brains evolved for our ability to survive on this planet. What purpose (meaning, what would be advantageous to our survival) would evolution have to grant us the ability to fully comprehend everything there is to know in the cosmos?

Surely, we must also understand that evidence has been accumulating on this planet for billions of years. Modern science has existed for a time period that is comparably not even a tiny droplet in the bucket of time. There is much left to be discovered in this world.

As we discover more and more, and God is removed from explanations more and more as a result, to what will theists turn as their evidence for God in the natural world?

"EVOLUTION IS JUST A THEORY"

I cannot even begin to remember the number of times I have heard this throughout my life. I have said it as well. As I now sat and read those words from a creationist, I felt humiliated for having ever said such words.

Gravity is a theory, too, yet those making this statement about evolution do not walk around with ropes holding their bodies to the ground for fear that they will float away into outer space and perish. The very thought is laughable.

In every day life, we often use the word theory to mean a guess or an idea. We use it when we are discussing an explanation that is possible, but we are unsure whether it is correct. However, scientists do not use the word theory in this manner.

When scientists discuss an idea or explanation that requires confirmation, it is called a hypothesis. A hypothesis is a statement that makes sense as a possibility based on the knowledge we currently have, but its truthfulness is still unknown and requires scientific testing.

A scientific theory, on the other hand, is an explanation of natural phenomena that has been repeatedly confirmed through scientific experimentation across multiple fields of science. A scientific theory has already been tested and confirmed extensively and is well-substantiated.

A scientific theory is not a guess or a proposition. It is not an idea awaiting confirmation. To say biological evolution is a scientific theory is to speak to the large amount of data consistently supporting it without any contradiction. It is hardly a valid attack.

I cringed as I saw creationist after creationist present this argument because I recalled the times I myself had presented it. I realized how ignorant and arrogant I had been. My hope for finding the answer I was searching for diminished the more I read.

THE MISSING LINK

I heard my entire childhood and adolescence that scientists had it wrong. We could not have descended from monkeys (I will address the claim that we came from monkeys shortly) because we do not have fossils linking humans to our ancestors. In other words, there are supposedly no fossilized remains of an intermediate species between our ancestors and us.

I believed this claim every time I had heard it. A friend of mine had even written a silly song about it, and I had often sang it while mocking evolutionary biologists. But, now, as I heard it once again in my pursuit for answers and clarity, I knew better. We absolutely have fossilized remains of many human-like, but not human, species.

We don't only have one or a few. We have thousands, and any of us is welcome to view them with full-colored pictures. They paint a beautiful and wonderful picture of our evolution, which took place over the course of around 7 million years. For more information, look over the Additional Reading section in the appendix.

For now, it is sufficient to say there is no missing link.

IF WE CAME FROM MONKEYS, WHY ARE THERE STILL MONKEYS?

First, we did not come from monkeys. Monkeys are our evolutionary cousins, not our direct ancestors. In other words, humans and monkeys share a common ancestor.

Secondly, as we can see from the information I provided about how new species form, you can easily see how one population may eventually evolve into a new species while the population from which it broke from does not. If the original population remains in a stable environment, it will change very little. Thus, it is entirely possible for a new species to form while the original species still remains.

Rather than helping me, these questions further revealed that the people I had looked to my entire life for truth were grossly misinformed. I felt angry that they had instructed me about my love for science and discovery and had made me feel so ashamed of myself when they did not know even the most rudimentary basics of science.

I realized how carelessly and irresponsibly they had acted toward me. If I were to advise someone on an issue, I should have at least a foundational knowledge about the issue at hand. I felt incredibly violated and betrayed.

Still, there was one point that was brought up to me that, while wrong, led me to a new idea which I thought might have merit.

"MR. SCIENTIST SAYS CREATIONISM IS THE TRUTH"

I had a couple scientists mentioned to me who were believers in creationism. Neither of those scientists were biologists. But, even if they were, what does this mean?

First, a scientific claim is not accepted as true simply because someone with a Ph.D. declares it to be so. This is not how science works. A scientific claim is accepted as very likely to be true upon the presentation of solid data to support that claim. Whether those data are presented by an individual holding a Ph.D. or an individual who is an undergraduate student is irrelevant. If there are data to support a claim, the claim is accepted.

These couple of scientists that have had their names tossed around to give some level of credence to creationism are obligated to provide solid data to support their claims. They cannot just flash a Ph.D. and say they are right.

If that were not true, and having a Ph.D. did mean a person is right, what about the millions of scientists across the world who each hold a Ph.D. and accept evolutionary theory? The discovery of truth involves not a competition of degrees and certifications but an evaluation of properly and meticulously collected data.

While none of these arguments satisfied me in the least, this last one segued into some claims that piqued my interest and grabbed my attention. I was presented with the idea of intelligent design. At first, it was quite alluring. I began to feel some hope.

I believed, for a time, that I had finally found the path toward reconciling my faith with my current knowledge, and I was thrilled. Perhaps I would need to adjust my previously held view about the Genesis account. I could live with that. What mattered to me at the time was that I could keep both scientific discovery and God.

I deeply desired to find evidence that this world was designed by God. I plunged into the claims of intelligent design head first, ready and excited to find God in the natural world. However, what I would find instead was immense disappointment and despair.

INTELLIGENT DESIGN

Intelligent design is a statement that the universe, or particularly, life on earth, could not have evolved by chance. It holds that an intelligent entity who serves as the creator or master designer is absolutely necessary for the world to exist as it does. It claims that living organisms are simply too complex to have evolved without the intervention of an intelligent being.

It is important to clarify that intelligent design is not a scientific theory, though it is often referred to as one. Remember that a scientific theory is an explanation for natural phenomena that has been repeatedly tested and consistently confirmed across multiple fields of science. Intelligent design does not meet this criteria.

Intelligent design is a statement of belief. It does not even qualify as a hypothesis. A hypothesis is based on the knowledge we currently have. However, intelligent design is not based on this. It is based only on the hopes and fantasies erected by our conceit.

My own hopes and fantasies led me to investigate these

claims. I hoped that the answer I was searching for would be found within them.

BY CHANCE?

Those who claim intelligent design do make one point that is absolutely true. The living organisms we see today could not have evolved by chance. But, no one is saying that they have. Evolution is not a process that happens through random chance.

The only random component of evolution is the genetic mutations that occur through errors made during the copying of DNA. That is where random chance happens, and that is where it ends.

However, natural selection is not random. Traits that are advantageous (and thus, the genes that code for them) show up more and more in a population, eventually changing the genetic make up of that population. That is not random.

Our bodies could not have just randomly fallen together. But, they could evolve through the non-random process of natural selection, given enough time. Evolution is not random. No one is claiming that it is.

As I began to sort through all of these claims presented to me, I began to realize how often evangelical Christians composed arguments against claims no one was even making in the first place. I have read entire essays about how impossible it is for human beings to have formed randomly when virtually no one in the sciences has even suggested that human beings did.

The ignorance about the topic from this group of people was radiating before my eyes. They were forming arguments against a scientific theory without even first learning about the theory itself. I realized I had been guilty of the same.

During Bible College, I spent a significant portion of my

science courses learning how to debunk evolutionary theory while learning absolutely nothing about evolutionary theory itself or the evidence for it. Now that I could see how grave of an error that was, I could no longer dismiss any claims without first learning about them.

So, in spite of these initial misunderstandings presented by proponents of intelligent design, I delved deeper into their claims. After all, I wanted them to be right.

THE DESIGNER

While the world is certainly full of wonder and joy, there is plenty here that is not particularly desirable. If we were to view the world as though it were designed by someone, what should we conclude about this designer?

How many people do you know in your life who have either chronic back problems or who have suffered a back injury of some kind? You likely know multiple people who have experienced this. Humans are quite prone to back injury.

Our spines are not an ideal design for walking upright. Our spines are quite similar to the spines of animals who walk on four legs except our bodies have a few modifications that make bipedal, upright walking possible. It works, yes.

If we were to design a human body from scratch, though, working on a drawing board, there would be much more suitable choices for a spine intended for upright walking. Those options would eliminate our tendency toward back injuries.

Evolution has to work with what is already there. It does not start from scratch. Standing upright allowed us to see both predators and prey more easily. Overall, this provided an advantage.

However, some individuals likely experienced back

injuries and lost their lives because of it. With evolution, a new trait can offer both disadvantages and advantages at the same time. Evolution often involves a compromise. As long as the advantages outweigh the disadvantages, though, the trait will be selected for.

Evolution does not have to be perfect. It simply requires that a trait causes a higher survival and reproduction rate than the rate of those without the trait.

We can excuse evolution for this as it is not a thinking, conscious being. I do not expect evolution to be driven by compassion and care as it is not conscious and aware. I do, however, expect that a conscious and intentional designer be driven by compassion and care.

What excuse would this designer have for being too lazy to come up with a design more fitting for upright walking rather than simply slapping a few modifications onto an already developed model and calling it a day? A friend of mine commented on the similarity of structures between different species. She explained that it was simply God using a good design over and over again.

This would make sense if these designs were all great in the scenarios in which we find them. But, they are not. Our spines are not a good design. And this is not the only example.

Let's look at more. Why create an opening to our bodies that is used for both breathing and eating? What a terrible idea. I recently read the story of a young boy who choked on some soup while eating his lunch. His mother desperately tried to save him as the paramedics rushed to help. However, the efforts failed, and he passed away.

What a cruel, monstrous beast one must be to stand back and watch a mother, in unimaginable agony, bury her child, knowing a better design that would have prevented the tragedy was available, but not chosen. How much less suffering would have happened in our world if we ate with one opening and breathed through another?

Consider a specific species of wasp that reproduces by stinging and paralyzing its prey and laying eggs inside its body. The animal then helplessly suffers as the larvae consume it from the inside out. It remains alive until the very end. What kind of a being would intentionally and knowingly create a means of reproduction such as this?

As the proponents of intelligent design claim that nature reveals to us the involvement of a creator, if we were to accept such a proposition, we would also have to accept what nature reveals about this creator. What we see is a creator who is apathetic, cruel, careless, and lazy. Any designer performing in this manner should be swiftly fired and sent on his way.

I reflected on this and understood that the excuse I had been given so often was not going to cut it for me any longer. None of this was made ok by the statement that this is the result of sin. To allow all of this suffering and death because two humans ate fruit from a forbidden tree made God appear so horrifyingly petty and sadistic.

Alternatively, the many examples I could give such as these make perfect sense in light of evolution, a process that happens naturally without intelligent thought or awareness. I would have no reason to expect care or compassion to be found in such a process.

OUR ORGANS ARE TOO COMPLEX TO HAVE EVOLVED?

I found proponents of intelligent design claiming that our organs are simply too complex to have come to exist through the process of natural selection alone. One common organ identified by these people is the eye.

The claim is that the eye is simply too complicated to have come to be through natural selection alone. It has too many different parts that work together to create sight for each of those parts to have evolved. Its complexity, they claim, is a sign of a creator or designer.

I decided to learn about the evolution of the eye to determine whether this were true. It turned out, we have a lot of information gleaned from tracing the development of the eye through natural selection. We can see its humble beginnings and its advancement to what we have today.

In more primitive species, such as starfish and leeches, eyes themselves are not present, but the surface of the body is slightly responsive to photons (particles of light), allowing the organisms to gain a tiny bit of information about the world around them. While the information is only a small amount, it is enough to provide an advantage.

As we move across the evolutionary line, we see gradual improvements in the pigment molecules through an increasing number of layers of pigment (the more layers, the more photons it can capture and thus, the more information it can receive). Every single layer of pigment added increases the ability to capture photons.

We can clearly see how this could gradually increase through the process of natural selection. If a mutation results in an organism having 41 layers rather than 40, it will have an advantage over the rest. The same goes for an organism having 2 layers rather than only one. Every additional layer provides an advantage.

An organism does not have to acquire 10 more layers at once in order to acquire an advantage. Nothing about this so far is complex, certainly not too complex to have occurred through natural selection.

This arrangement of photocells provides information about the environment, but does not give the organism any information about the location or direction from which the light traveled. However, if a dark screen is behind one side of the photocells, this allows for a rudimentary way of determining the direction from which the light is coming. The organism must swing its head from side to side to ascertain this information, but the point is it can obtain that information, which provides an advantage.

The need to move one's head from side to side is eliminated if the photocells are then on a curved surface rather than a flat one. The curved surface means the photocells are facing different directions, which means they are now capable of sensing the direction light is traveling. Now, this information can be obtained more easily.

A little bit of curvature allows for a little more ease in obtaining this information. A little bit more curvature allows for even more. And a little bit more curvature allows for yet even more ease. Again, we see how tiny, gradual changes bring advantages, step by step.

As the curvature continues more and more, and the cup shape it produces gets deeper and deeper, it will eventually reach the point in which it has curved completely around and the opening is only the size of a pinhole. At this point, an actual image can now be seen by the organism.

Now, the organism does not simply have information that there is light and from where it is coming. It has an image of what is actually there, albeit a very rudimentary image (due to so little light entering the eye, the image will be rather dark, not one that is perfectly clear).

If something were to exist over the hole, however, even a jelly-like substance, the light would be more focused, producing a sharper image. This does not require a fully formed lens. Anything that focuses the light will work enough to provide an advantage. Indeed, there are animals even today with a "lens" that is essentially an extremely thin glob of jelly.

From there, any mutation that allows for an even more focused image will provide a further advantage, so the lens will improve its ability to create a sharp image more and more through small, gradual changes to it.

Now, imagine the arrival of the ability to ever so slightly change the size of the hole through which light enters. Even a small amount of this ability provides an advantage. When it is darker, the hole will allow just a little more light in, and when it is light, the hole will allow just a little bit less.

When an individual is born with just a little bit more of this ability, that provides an advantage. And then, a little bit more ability provides even more of an advantage. These rudimentary pupils eventually become better at opening more or less in response to more or less light.

I could continue on, but I believe the point has been made. The human eye is not too complex to have developed through natural selection. We can see how even very minor changes offered an advantage to organisms, and the slow accumulation of those traits eventually led to the eyes you are using to read this book.

There is much more to be said about the evolution of eyes. As I have mentioned before, I have offered a suggested reading list in the appendix, and if you desire to learn more detailed information, I recommend looking through that list and giving some of those books a read. In Richard Dawkins' Climbing Mount Improbable, he offers an explanation that is much more detailed and eloquent regarding the evolution of the eye than what I have offered here.

For our purposes, we can see how natural selection resulted in the eyes you and I use every day. There is and never was a need for an intelligent being to intervene with this process. Natural selection was sufficient to do so on its own.

This argument about the eye was one of the pillars of intelligent design. After doing my research, I could see that their argument was incorrect. The only people I knew who believed this argument knew almost nothing about evolutionary theory. It seemed to be an idea that required its followers to be ignorant of the facts.

A similar argument intelligent designers offer is that our vital organs could not have evolved because they are dependent on one another. My heart will stop working if I do not have a functioning kidney, and my kidneys will stop working if I do not have a functioning heart. Therefore, they could not have evolved, according to this argument, because they both would have had to come into existence together at the same time.

I sat one afternoon and considered this. I had learned enough about natural selection at that point to be able to think it through on my own. I realized that for one to offer such a suggestion demonstrates a profound misunderstanding of evolutionary theory.

Suppose an organism has a very rudimentary heart. The organism is extremely small, and therefore, a very primitive pump is sufficient to produce some movement of materials around in the organism. Such a primitive pump would not require a filtration system (a kidney) in order to work.

In a future generation, the very beginnings of a filtration system would provide an advantage to the organism so when it appeared, it took hold. If something toxic comes along and there is something there to filter at least some of it out of the organism, that would be an advantage. Perhaps that filter does need the pump so the material can get to the filter. But, the pump was there, which allowed this advantage to take hold.

Much further down the road, both that pump and that filter can improve through the process of natural selection. If the pump gains an advantage that requires the filter to be present in order to work, that's quite alright because the filter is there. Likewise, if the filter gains an advantage that requires the pump to be present in order to work, that's alright as well because the pump is there.

Over time, the evolution of these organs includes changes that require both the pump and filter until finally, we have kidneys and a heart that are dependent on one another. The first primitive pump could and did work without the filter, but the heart we see in many species today cannot function without the kidney because they evolved together, step by step, in the presence of one another.

This same explanation could be made for any of our vital organs. They are dependent on one another in their current form indeed, but that does not mean they were always dependent on one another from the very beginning. Each organ could take on an advantage that required an accompanying organ whenever that accompanying organ was there.

I knew this argument of the intelligent designers made no sense. But, I read on. I wanted to find something that would make sense and offer some hope.

THE CAMBRIAN EXPLOSION

Many proponents of intelligent design claim that the "Cambrian explosion" is evidence of creation. They claim we cannot find any fossils that date prior to the Cambrian period (about 500 million years ago). They further claim that fossils of all major groups appeared very suddenly, which is further evidence of creation.

I had learned a lot at that point about the Cambrian period and the Cambrian explosion. There was definitely diversification that happened during this period. But, the same is true for many time periods of similar length since then. I knew it is not the case that the species that appeared in the Cambrian period showed up all at once. This diversification occurred over the span of 80 million years. That is hardly supportive of the Genesis one narrative.

Before this period, species were much more primitive and small. So small, in fact, they were microscopic. This is why, for a long time, we could not find any fossils from the pre-Cambrian period. We weren't looking for them in the right way.

However, since the 1940s, we have discovered more and more fossils that pre-date the Cambrian period, and we now have an abundance of them. Life absolutely existed on earth prior to this time period.

Intelligent design proponents often use quotes from scientists that they claim support their explanation of the Cambrian period, but these quotes are routinely from very old sources, made when we did not know as much as we now know. As I have already mentioned, as more is discovered, our scientific understanding is improved upon and corrected.

This is in stark contrast to a creationist posing as a scientist who turns to quotes that are decades old and refuses to let them go because they can twist them to support their view. These individuals are counting on the ignorance of their audience so their words will be accepted without question. The entire proposition seemed to be built on a foundation of deceit.

The more I explored, the more I saw that intelligent design is not based on scientific data, but on ignorance. Anyone who actually knows the scientific data would see that the arguments presented by intelligent designers are in contradiction of all of the data we currently have.

PRE-CONCEIVED IDEAS

There was a primary difference I found between intelligent designers and the field of science as whole. Proponents of intelligent design had decided going in what they already believed to be true. They then viewed all evidence through the lens of that predetermined view. They scoured the data for anything that could possibly be twisted around to use as evidence for their beliefs and ignored everything else.

Those engaging in real science, on the other hand, do not determine their conclusions until after they have properly evaluated scientific data. Equally as significant, they are always willing to change their minds if new data are ever presented that show the current thinking had gotten it wrong.

An inquiry is not science if it is approached with a predetermined set of beliefs. Preconceived ideas do not belong anywhere in science. Donald Prothero said it best in his book, Evolution: What the Fossils Say and Why it Matters,

> *"If we want them* [our conclusions] *to make sense and not violate what we have learned about nature, we have to be true to the conclusions to which nature leads us. We cannot twist and bend our explanations into pretzels...just to save some cherished belief."*

I love science. I appreciated the humility and willingness to change that I had had the opportunity to observe amongst those in this field. After living around people who were certain to have all the answers and who were unwilling to learn anything new, this component of the field of science was one I cherished. But, I did not see this cherished component among those who subscribed to the idea of intelligent design.

Intelligent design was the one hope I had to reconcile the

knowledge I had gained with my faith, and it had failed. It had failed miserably. Those in my faith that I had approached with questions had not been able to provide a single satisfactory answer.

I only knew one final place to turn. I turned to the Bible, God's word. My eyes were about to be opened, and I would never be able to close them again.

THE REAL BIBLE

During my first semester as a full-time student, I had enrolled, along with other introductory courses, in a history class. In retrospect, I'm thankful, believe it or not, that none of my credits transferred from the Bible college I had attended even though that meant I had to retake basic freshman and sophomore courses in a variety of subjects.

Similar courses I had taken in Bible college were very limited and biased in their scope, presenting only views that were in line with our faith. There were huge portions of these various subjects that I had not been exposed to. Receiving an education through starting completely over again offered me the opportunity to gain a more complete picture of these various subjects of study.

In my history course, I read a letter written by a high ranking member of the Spanish army to the King of Spain, communicating how things were going after their arrival in the Americas. According to the letter writer, things were going quite well, and God was the one he credited for it.

He wrote about how easily the "savages" had been slain as they had no guns or swords. He spoke of a field covered in slaughtered Indians and running over with their blood. He spoke of many Indians writhing around on the field in agony as they died with both of their arms severed from their bodies.

This was good news, he said. He offered praise and gratefulness to God for showing his mighty hand and granting them victory. It was an incredibly appalling letter that would make most anyone's stomach turn.

This was not the God I knew. The God I served was a God of peace. He loved everyone with a love we could not comprehend. Not even the love of a mother for her child could compare. God would never be pleased with such an event.

Or would he?

IN THE BEGINNING...

I opened my Bible, determined to find the answers for my confusion directly from the word of God to finally put my soul at peace. I began at the very beginning. "In the beginning, God created the heavens and the earth."

I read the account of creation, which I now knew was not true. I tried to believe it. But, I had learned too much, and one cannot unlearn information. I knew it was impossible for this story to be accurate, but maybe it was just an allegory to show God created the world. I justified it through such thoughts, and moved forward.

I then read the story of Adam and Eve. I had read that story many times before in depth, studying each and every aspect. It had never sounded so silly to me as it did now. A woman was made from a man's rib? Why would God have to use a rib at all?

He spoke the entire cosmos into existence, but he couldn't manage to create a woman without having material to work with? As a young child, while I attended an evangelical Christian school, I was taught in my science classes that girls have one more rib than boys because Adam had one of his ribs removed to make a woman.

Of course, this is completely untrue. Men and women have the same number of ribs. This is not to mention that even if a man did have a rib removed due to an accident or surgical intervention, this does not mean all males born in his line would then be missing a rib while all females born in his line would have all of the original human ribs.

A talking snake spoke with Eve. Christians will defend this explaining that it was the devil disguising himself as a snake. It was not an actual snake. If that were true, wouldn't Eve still have been shocked to hear a snake talking?

If a snake slithered up to me and struck up a conversation, I dare say I hope someone will call the nearest mental health institution so they can provide me with needed medical treatment. But, Eve just continued with the conversation as though nothing unusual was going on.

Are we at all surprised that Eve was the one to initiate the fall of man? This fits well with a book which declares that men are meant to lead and women require the direction of men. There is a woman with a rather large following on the internet who teaches women how to be godly women based on the instructions of the Bible.

According to her, women are intended to marry and bear children. Their husband is to be in charge of everything, and women are to obey without question. If the husband desires to have sex, and the woman is ill, tired, or just not in the mood, it is her obligation to provide her husband with sexual intercourse regardless.

She claims that when a man cheats, it is the woman's fault for not providing appropriate sexual satisfaction to her husband. Men, she claims, absolutely must have sex, and if they are not getting enough of it at home, they have no choice but to seek it elsewhere. I must say I am not particularly fond of the idea of giving total control of my life to someone who has no control whatsoever over his penis.

Women are not to question the decisions of their husbands. They are to be quiet and serve their husbands. They are to be thoughtless, obedient minions to the men of this world. Looking at what the Bible says, that pretty much is accurate with the teachings of the Scripture. Some will point out the few instances in the Bible in which a woman provided wisdom or some other leadership role.

Overall, however, the directions for women are indeed to quietly submit to their husbands and obey them. Women are not to instruct a man. Women are to be silent in the church. That is what the Bible says, and I've heard some doozies from Christians attempting to explain those verses away.

Now, I could see how the Bible really presents women. Women were the ultimate reason for the fall. The lesson is clear from the beginning of the book about what happens to women without a man right there to direct them. I felt sickened.

THE GREAT FLOOD

According to the Bible, just 6,000 years or so ago, the entire world was covered with water, even the highest peaks of the mountain. Where did all of that water come from? It could not possibly have been floating around in the atmosphere. Even if it were entirely saturated, the atmosphere could not hold anywhere near that amount of water.

After the flood, where did all that water go? It could not have simply evaporated. As I just said, the atmosphere cannot hold anywhere near that amount of water.

The number of animals that would have had to fit on the

ark was also not possible. The dimensions of the ark are given in the Bible. Many creationists claim that it was not two of every species that boarded the ark, but two of every "kind" of animal. Then, after the flood, the "kinds" diversified from there into the variety we see today.

That scenario would require extremely rapid natural selection in order to occur. Natural selection does not work that quickly. Remember as I explained the Cambrian explosion, I mentioned that diversification happened over tens of millions of years, and that is considered fairly rapid. Diversification to that extent in 6,000 years? No.

The geological evidence we would find from a flood like this so recently in the earth's history would be clear and profound. Yet, no one has ever found a single piece of evidence that indicates there was ever a flood like this.

Some creationists claim the Grand Canyon is evidence of Noah's flood. There are many pieces of evidence found in the Grand Canyon that actually show it was not ever exposed to such a catastrophic flood. The layers of sedimentation show a very long history through which this canyon slowly formed.

There were times that it was wet with river waters, and there were times it was dry like a desert. We see this diverse history in its individual layers. None of this happened over the course of a year-long, worldwide flood.

I began to think about the moral implications of this story. According to the story, God drowned infants, toddlers, young children, and droves of animals. The Bible states this is because the world had become so evil. But, God was all powerful. He was so powerful, he could speak the entire cosmos into existence from nothing.

Was there not another way? God, who is capable of anything, had no other option than drowning everyone? At the very least, even if these people had to die, hypothetically, couldn't he have just allowed them to pass peacefully in their sleep?

Did they, including children and babies, really have to experience the sheer terror of massive amounts of rain falling from the sky until it overtook them and drowned them? I had been taught that God is merciful and kind. Nothing about this story made God appear to be either.

What about the animals? They are considered morally neutral. Animals do not sin and do not have souls. Yet, they all suffered such a terrible fate due to the sin of man. How is that right or fair? This thought led me further into the Old Testament, and I was now able to read it with fresh eyes.

AN ONGOING ANGER MANAGEMENT PROBLEM

God had always been presented to me as an all-loving, all-powerful God. He gave his only son so we could go to heaven. He loved us more than anyone else ever could.

Of course, I knew about the stories of the Old Testament. I knew about the wars and the slayings. But, they had always been justified to me as acts that had to be carried out because the people would not turn from their evil ways.

I had never really thought about it very deeply. I barely even thought of those people as people. They were Hittites, Amorites, Canaanites…not people. Now, as I read the Scripture, I read about them, understanding more clearly that if those stories were true, these things were done to actual people.

Orders from God included ripping pregnant women to shreds, slamming infants into rocks, and running swords through little children. If God was willing to go after infants and young children, he certainly had no problem with raining his fury onto the innocent.

God selected specific punishments for not obeying him,

and those punishments were severe. Moses had a fleeting moment of doubt and was forbidden entrance to the Promised Land as a result. This story of Moses' doubt had been drilled into me from a young age. We must never doubt, not even for a moment. To do so even for just a second would lead to disastrous consequences.

Meanwhile, never mind that Moses had instructed the Israelites to go to war and kill everyone except the virgin women. The virgin women were to be kept so the Israelites could rape and enslave them. God was willing to give that a pass. But, doubt in God's instructions, even for a moment? Unacceptable.

The more I read, the more it became clear just how easy it was to piss God off. This was not a mild-mannered, stable being. The kinds of orders he gave would give no other indication than a severe case of psychopathy. This guy was nuts.

I had never seen a better example of an individual, whether human or otherwise, with an ongoing anger management problem. Every time someone offended him, he would completely lose it and lash out. The end result was typically rivers of blood, including the blood of babies and children. Hitler sounded more gentle than this God.

I began to wonder, what if I had been born before Jesus Christ? I was currently struggling with doubts, and I was fighting them with all I could. Yet, the doubts were still there. Would God have struck me, too?

Would he have sent someone to slaughter me with a sword? Would he have refused me entrance to a land he had promised was for me and my family?

What if I, a non-Jew, would have been born back then? Would God have cared about me at all? As I read the rules of God's people in the Old Testament, the answer to that question became clear. I wasn't sure God cared about any of those people, Israelite or not.

THE RULES

The rules of the Old Testament are extremely bizarre. If a man rapes a woman, he is to pay money to her father and then, marry her. This woman, who has already endured a rape, not only is not compensated in any way, but she must now marry her rapist and continue to be raped by him throughout her life.

I mentioned this to a friend of mine, telling her I was completely bewildered by such an instruction. She explained, "You have to understand the time period in which God made these rules. Back then, if a woman was raped, a man would not want anything to do with her. She would never marry, which means she would have no way of surviving because women were financially dependent on men."

My mouth was hanging open. This was the justification? I replied, "So, if God was speaking to people and instructing them regarding how to live, why wouldn't he just say don't treat women this way? Why not say to not put women in a position where they have to have a man to survive? Don't treat a woman who was raped as though she is dirty and unworthy of marriage or love. That's what he should have said."

She had no response. Who would? Are we to truly believe that God had to water things down to make goodness more palatable to his primitive followers and that he was perfectly willing to do so? We can't have even a moment of doubt or we will suffer the consequences, but true justice for rape victims...that apparently could wait a few millennia until people had a better grasp of women's rights?

The punishment for worshipping another God or working on the Sabbath was death. But, the punishment for rape was a handful of silver coins and a marriage. I was appalled.

Slavery is approved of in the Old Testament, and rules for slave owners are listed there. Would not a better rule have been to just not own slaves? Perhaps if God had commanded the Israelites to not own slaves and to never treat a human being like property, slavery would not have gone on for so long in America.

The Bible was often used to justify the practice of slavery as moral and right. If God, they figured, who is all loving and merciful had no problems with slavery, then, surely slavery was right and good. In their minds, by abducting people from their homes and auctioning them off like you would a piece of furniture, they were simply carrying out God's will as described in the holy Bible.

I've had people tell me, in their attempts to soften this reality, that many abolitionists were inspired by the Bible to fight against and end slavery. Sure, but the reality is that had those Scripture verses about slavery not been there in the first place, and instead, a commandment forbidding slavery been there instead, maybe those abolitionists could have spent their lives pursuing justice in another area because slavery would have already been abolished.

The only acceptable rule for slavery is that it should not be practiced. Yet, you will not find such a rule or commandment anywhere in the Bible, the supposed moral guide for us all.

THE JUDGE

The only way anyone could receive forgiveness, according to the Old Testament, was through the blood of an animal. Animals who had done no wrong were to be sacrificed or even sent off into the wilderness to slowly starve to death in agony. Then, forgiveness would be offered to the person making the sacrifice.

For most people, an apology is sufficient if they have been offended, assuming the apology is sincere. For God, however, he was far too angry for such an arrangement. He demanded blood.

Why? If God is in charge of everything, why not choose a different means of forgiveness? Inevitably, Christians remind us that this is not a sign of God's anger or moral failing because God ultimately sent his only son to die and shed his innocent blood so that no other sacrifices would be required.

Let's think about this, though. Imagine a man on trial for murder. The evidence against him is strong. There is video evidence through which we can observe him committing the violent act. His fingerprints, hair, and blood were found at the scene and on the victim. There is no doubt he has committed this murder.

So, the jury convicts him and declares him guilty. The day comes for the sentencing from the judge, and as the murderer awaits his sentence, another man runs into the courthouse. This man falls before the judge and gives an intense, emotional plea, explaining that he loves the convicted murderer with all of his being, and he cannot bear to see him imprisoned.

With tears streaming down his face, he begs the judge to allow the murderer to go free. The judge explains he cannot do so because doing so would violate the basic principle of justice. The man looks around the courtroom. He looks at the murderer and to the people sitting in the seats behind him who were waiting to hear the sentence.

He looks back to the judge and speaks. "Please, let me carry out his sentence in his place."

The judge shrugs his shoulders. "Alright. The murderer will be set free. You, sir, are sentenced to life in prison."

Who would actually go for this? While it may say something about the man who sacrificed himself for the person he loves, let's look at what this says about the judge. The judge had just indicated that it does not matter who is punished for a crime, as long as someone is punished.

If someone you loved was murdered, would you be satisfied with an innocent person being jailed for the crime? Would that be just? Would you not be outraged to learn that a judge had allowed your loved one's murderer to run free, agreeing to sentence an innocent man in the murderer's place?

Nothing about this makes any sense whatsoever, yet it is the foundation of the Christian faith. We are cursed because of the sin of someone else. We are depraved and incapable of not committing sins. God then demands punishment be thrust onto an innocent, sin-less being so he can forgive those sins.

Understanding what even the sacrifice of Jesus Christ says about God rendered the New Testament an appalling testimony of the character of this God. I had spent my life hearing of this loving, righteous God. But, as I read the Bible now with fresh eyes, I could not find this loving, righteous God there.

I had looked to the Bible to find answers. The answers it revealed were quite different than what I'd been hoping to find.

TRANSFORMATION

I wrestled. I fought. I agonized. What was I going to do? I wanted my faith. I wanted it to work. But, everything I had come to know had slowly chiseled it down, little by little, until there was nothing left but a bleeding nub.

I often lay awake at night, wondering how I could manage life without God. While I had not admitted it to myself yet, deep down, I understood that there was no going back.

How could I make my faith continue to work in spite of what I now knew and understood? I was terrified. I had never considered life without this close, personal God. God had been my best friend through the darkest of nights. He had gone with me everywhere. He knew exactly who I was and accepted me in spite of it. How could I live life without him?

My fear of the unknown gripped the core of my being. Could I accept that this God I had come to know, love, and serve had never actually been there? The grief and loss I imagined for myself was incomprehensible. The most defining quality of my entire life and my entire world as I had come to know it would be gone.

I earnestly prayed, asking God to show himself to me in some way. My prayers continued to be answered with silence. I begged. I pleaded. There was no revelation, no sign or hint that this deep desire of mine made any difference at all in the universe.

My heart was breaking. I was in terrible pain. I had no idea how to move forward.

Then, it all changed. I found a satirical website titled Landover Baptist Church. It is still around today and can be found through a simple Google search. The website pretended to function as the website of an evangelical Christian church. Through humor and shocking bluntness, it exposed the absurdities of the evangelical Christian faith.

At the time, there were audio sermons, and I listened to them again and again for days. I read the articles. I laughed. I cried. Then, I laughed some more.

I began to see that I wasn't crazy. These beliefs really were absurd. I was not having these doubts because I was defective in some way. I was simply seeing the truth after being blinded from it for so many years.

The ability of these writers to bring humor to my situation allowed me to see that were I to leave this faith, somehow, I would be alright. I expected it to be awful if I were to do so, but yet, I now understood that I would get through it.

I had been walking around with a gaping, raw wound that caused me tremendous pain each and every day. The laughter I found from this satirical website provided the bandage and soothing ointment I needed. It allowed me to open myself to the possibility that this wound could heal if I gave it a chance.

Finally, at long last, I sat in my bedroom one mid afternoon with tears streaming down my face. My heart felt as though it were about to explode. My hands shook. I knew what was about to happen. I had come to understand. I no longer believed. I had been trying to the best of my ability, but it was not enough.

The Bible assured me that if I had faith the size of a mustard seed, I could use it to move mountains. I had pressed, pulled, and struggled as I hung onto my mustard seed-sized faith, but the mountain I had furiously and violently attempted to move had not budged.

It was over. I was about to accept that my faith was and had always been untrue and end my struggle once and for all. I prepared to endure the most terribly intense grief I had ever experienced. I waited for the sheer terror of what this would mean for my future to thrust itself into me and suffocate all happiness from my life. I wondered how I would manage to build a new life without God. Yet, I knew I would have to.

I took a deep breath, and, without giving it any further thought, I acknowledged and fully accepted what I had already come to know. The God of the Bible, the close, personal, loving Savior around whom my entire life had always revolved, did not exist. He had never existed. Through it all, it had been in my imagination. None of it had been real.

When I thought God had revealed himself to me during that first week at youth camp, it had simply been the music and smooth words that had manipulated my emotional experiences. When I believed I had been filled with the Holy Spirit and God had answered my prayers, I had actually just been muttering gibberish.

When I knelt in my seat during a youth group service and answered the call to ministry, there had never been such a call. I had simply fallen for the pressures to do so while I was young and vulnerable. God had never selected me for a special purpose to further his kingdom. God had not done so because he was not even there.

God had been nothing more than an imaginary friend. Any comfort I received from him was a fantasy. None of it had been real, not a single moment. I audibly spoke. "It wasn't real. None of it."

I waited for the grief to wash over me. I prepared myself for the agonizing terror and sense of loss that would surely burst from the depths of my being. Would I feel the need to throw myself to the floor in anguish? Would I sit and weep? Would I vomit? I was not sure. I only knew it was going to be horrible.

Then, to my extreme astonishment, I realized I did not feel horrible. I felt no grief at all. I felt no fear. There was no anguish or agony. There were no tears. There was no vomiting or pains of the stomach. None of the terrible feelings I had thought would now rule my existence happened at all. In fact, I felt the exact opposite of all I had anticipated.

I was overtaken with an exuberant joy. It were as though the sun had risen for the very first time. I wanted jump to my feet and dance in sheer exhilaration at the discovery of my newfound autonomy. I had never felt so light and so free.

When I had declared my non belief, God had not vanished from my life alone. All that my religion had taught me about myself and the world vanished along with him. When all of that disappeared, my very need for this God ceased that very instant.

My faith had taught me that I was born evil, dark, and depraved. It had told me I was worthless and deserving of only eternal torture and punishment. I was unlovable and ugly. There was nothing good about me. The only goodness that could be found within me was the goodness God brought with him when he entered my black heart. God loved me in spite of my unlovableness.

Now, I could see that I was not evil, dark, and depraved. I did not deserve eternal torture and punishment. The goodness within myself was truly a part of me. I did not have a black heart. I held beauty. I was precious not because someone else made me so but simply because I was.

The mere thought was elating. I could enjoy myself and take delight in myself for the first time in my entire life. I did not need a savior for I did not need saved. Darkness did not hold me in its clutches. There was no need for rescue.

My life was mine and mine alone. I was able to make my own decisions. I was able to plan my own life without requiring permission from a higher being.

Unbeknownst to me, this God had made me feel hideous and atrocious. This God had kept me in bondage. Now, it was finally over. Like a battered woman who had just escaped the rule and control of her abusive lover, I was free. God had been the problem all along, not me.

The revelation did not stop there. I looked out through my bedroom window to observe the world. I had always believed it was a place of suffering and pain. I would sing songs declaring this world was not my home. It was a mere temporary place until I reached my true home.

Now, I suddenly understood that this world was indeed my home. It was the only home I had ever known, and it was the only home I ever would know. And, even better, it was not a place of only suffering and pain. It was also filled with immense beauty, and I was a part of that beauty.

I had believed that God made us separate from the animals. Animal were lowly creatures, and we humans were far superior as we all but owned the world. I had believed that everything in the world had been created specifically for humans and that the world was all about us.

As that arrogance melted from my shoulders, I saw that other organisms on earth did not exist for me. They existed in this world in their own right and for their own reasons. They carried beauty of their own, not for me, but for their own selves.

We had all descended from the same spark of life that had occurred so very long ago. Whether close or distant, we were all kin. A feeling of peace, harmony, and connection to the magnificence and wonder of the world flowed like a river through my mind and heart.

I considered how much had to happen in a specific manner for me to have ever even existed at all. It had not been a plan by a supreme being, and my existence now displayed itself as all the more miraculous. I thought of everything that had to happen over the course of billions of years in just a certain way so that at a particular moment in time, my parents would come together and that egg and that sperm would combine to create me.

The thought that someone would be here right now is not particularly stunning. However, the thought that I was lucky and fortunate enough for it to have been me was dizzyingly exciting. How many other potential lives never were and never will be? But, I get to exist as a conscious being. I get to experience life while so many others did not and never will.

I considered the portions of this world that are indeed filled with sorrow and pain. Before, I believed starving children all went to heaven, so it was not overly bothersome that such a thing happened. A pit in my stomach rose. What if starving children go no where? What if this is their one and only chance to experience any happiness at all and instead, they experience only pain?

The value of life soared immensely. For everyone here, this is it. It is the sole opportunity to experience joy. How exorbitantly tragic it is every single time life was lost prematurely or filled with suffering and agony. Life is so incredibly precious and valuable.

I strongly desired to do what I could to reduce the suffering of others in this world. I felt more motivated to do so than I ever had before. Such an endeavor is not a meaningless or purposeless pursuit.

I had thought my life would mean so much less to me if I ceased to believe in the God I had once served. Instead, my life came to mean so much more. Others came to mean so much more. The world came to mean so much more.

Most of all, I did not need God to give me or my life meaning. My experiences mattered simply because they had meaning to me. And that was enough.

There would be no more kneeling. Never again would I bow myself down before another. I was in charge of my own life. I was the one who could decide what my life would mean and accomplish. It was all in my grasp.

I breathed in the world and all of its glory. I opened my arms and embraced its loveliness. An extraordinary level of peace and contentment settled into my soul. I was whole. I was fulfilled. I was satisfied.

And...I was an atheist.

A FOREIGN WORLD

As all of this was happening, social media was just beyond its infancy. Many of my friends whom I had known since I was a child were online, and we communicated regularly. I was fearful of the consequences of coming out and telling everyone what I had decided was the truth. So, I kept it hidden and did not directly share my newfound freedom with those I loved.

However, the change that had occurred within me showed itself in other ways. A couple people mentioned that a member of our youth group we had been friends with as teenagers had come out as gay.

I was disgusted with their sneers and judgmental remarks. He was my friend, and I cared about him. It would be wrong to go along with their comments or to say nothing. So, I spoke up and defended him.

He has the right to live a life that is true to himself, and who are we to determine he should do otherwise, I explained. He was happy and with the person he loved. Was that not what mattered? None of them were pleased with my input.

I had spent years as a member of the religious right. Now, unlike my friends, I was quite a bit more liberal on several issues. My comments on social or political issues being discussed amongst my friends were met with disdain. The gap between my friends and I was widening, and they noticed.

Over the course of a few months, my friends list had dwindled to very small remnant. My friends had abandoned me. People whom I had known and loved since I was a young child no longer wanted anything to do with me. I had simply been written off.

I heard through my few remaining friends that others were being told to stay away from me because I had been brainwashed by liberals and by demons. I had given up the anointing of God, and I was a dangerous influence.

Others said they felt angry whenever they spoke to me because I shared a different view than their own, so they did not wish to speak with me any longer. This was very difficult for me to understand. I had never once been rude or abrasive toward any of them. I had simply responded to questions or discussions they had started and shared my thoughts on the subject at hand.

Many found this sharing of my thoughts to be enraging. I was deeply hurt. I had known these people most my life. Some were almost like family to me. I had hoped we could weather through the changes brought about by my new perspective because our friendship was so valuable. Apparently, it was not that valuable to them after all.

Soon, nearly everyone was gone. I was alone.

I was very busy with school and with work. I was working two jobs in the field of science to pay the bills for my tiny, city apartment. I loved what I was doing each day. But, I was incredibly, devastatingly lonely.

I grieved terribly. I tried to reach out to my former

friends on occasion and share how hurt I was by their treatment of me. No one ever replied. For the first time, I was experiencing what the love of evangelical Christianity really involves. It is conditional and easily thrown away.

SINCERE FAITH, INSINCERE LOVE

The true love of evangelical Christians is their dogma, and anyone who interferes with that is swiftly removed and not seriously thought of ever again. While I cannot know for sure how these former friends were feeling, the appearance they gave was that I was not even missed. That aspect was the most difficult to cope with.

If I was not missed, had I really been enjoyed? Was I even loved by them at all or had it all been a charade?

I had worked through the realization that none of my interactions with God had been real. Now, I was realizing none of my interactions with my friends had been real, either. If my political opinions or beliefs about the truthfulness of a religion were enough to erase me from their lives without giving it a second thought, I surely was never loved by them to begin with.

As I worked through my pain, I pondered the idea that perhaps, deep down, I had always known their love for me was not authentic. After all, if I truly believed I was loved by them, why was I so afraid to ask them about my questions regarding speaking in tongues when I was in high school? I was fearful of rejection for simply asking honest questions.

I realized they had never loved me for who I am. When my love for science was observed, I was not fully accepted. I was pushed to turn from those desires so I would become more like the person they wanted me to be. Otherwise, I would not have been accepted from the start.

I had never been able to ask questions about our faith or

truly be myself. It was the only reason those friendships had survived as long as they did. They did not wish to support me doing what made me happy. They had never been true friends all along.

While this new understanding brought me a small level of comfort as it explained that I had not lost as much as it felt I had lost, my emotions still remained paralyzed in grief. While I knew it is better to have no friends than fake friends, I still missed them all very much.

I missed chatting on the phone during a long drive home from school or work. When something funny happened, I would reach for the phone to call the person I knew would find it humorous only to remember that friend was not talking to me anymore and would not answer the phone if I was the one calling.

In spite of the hustle and bustle of the city, my days seemed overwhelmed by silence. It was unbearable. I recognized it was time to accept what had happened and develop some new, more authentic friendships.

STARTING OVER

I began attempting to socialize with my fellow students and employees. I struggled with this much more than I had anticipated I would. I had lived my entire life mostly separate from the outside world, and evangelical Christians as a whole behave quite differently from non-evangelical Christians.

I am not referring here to their religious beliefs. It runs deeper than that. The sense of humor of the average evangelical Christian differs from what you find among people outside of that faith. Activities enjoyed by typical evangelical Christians are very different from those enjoyed by non-evangelical Christians. They talk differently. They do things differently.

I did not know how to interact with people outside of the faith I had left. They never laughed at my jokes, and I rarely understood the humor behind their jokes. References to music groups and movies were over my head for I had not listened to secular music at any point in my life, and I rarely had watched movies.

Often, conversations revolved around a story that had happened in the past, but I was too uncomfortable to share my past with others. During such conversations, I remained quiet.

I did not want to be known as the ex-evangelical Christian. That religion had consumed enough of my identity as it was. I was not going to give it any more of myself.

I also felt embarrassed. Now that I could see the absurdity of the beliefs I had once held so dear, I did not know how I could share them with others without being treated as though I were odd or strange. What if I revealed this part of myself and they laughed at me?

I desperately tried to make new friends, but failed miserably. Weeks passed and then, months passed. I had not made a single friend. I could not remember the last time I had engaged in a social activity of any kind. Loneliness was with me everywhere I went.

I did not know how to deal with it. In the past, every time a problem arose, I simply knelt down to pray. I would ask God for help. That was how we were taught to deal with every issue. Without prayer, I was not sure what else to do.

The loneliness persistently reminded me of the friendships I once had, but had lost. I watched movies alone in my apartment. I went out to eat by myself. I was always alone.

One night, the loneliness and pain became so great, I cried as

I rested my head on my pillow to get some rest. I wanted to be cared about. I wanted to have someone else to care about. Even just one or two friends would be enough. I just needed someone.

Dating was not a simple path, either. I was extremely sexually inexperienced. At my age, the world of dating was very difficult under such circumstances. The very prospect of meeting someone who would understand where I was in life seemed impossible.

I did not feel I could continue to live my life like this. Something had to give. Somehow, I had to make new friends. I needed community. There was only one way I knew to achieve this goal.

BACKSLIDING

I returned to church. I went to a few churches of a more progressive Christian faith, but found I did not fit well there. I ran into much of the same social awkwardness and difficulties I had found outside of my former faith. I then decided to try out an evangelical Christian church located around the corner from my apartment.

I knew I would never be able to believe the teachings of this church. However, I wondered if I could accept a more watered down version of Christianity. Perhaps even though the Bible was not true, there were important lessons to be learned from it. Maybe I could focus on those lessons, disregard everything else, and find a way to make it work.

I began attending on Sunday mornings. As the music was played and the people around me worshipped, I felt a pit in my stomach. I did not want to engage. It was not real. I was incredibly uncomfortable as though I were revisiting a traumatic experience from my past.

Sometimes, I enjoyed the sermons. Other times, I was wrought with disgust as I listened to them. Messages were preached from the pulpit declaring homosexuals as people deceived by the devil.

Shouts of support flew from the congregation to the stage. "Amen!"

"Hallelujah, brother!"

I was sitting amongst a bunch of bigots. I myself had once been a bigot, and I refused to ever go back. I felt out of place.

I was eventually invited to attend a Bible study that consisted of single women. I attended only once. I have no memory of the subject matter of discussion that evening. I only remember one statement made by the study's leader.

"It's like evolution, you know, which has just no evidence for it whatsoever!"

Everyone laughed with her and mocked scientists and all who accepted evolutionary theory. I sat quietly in the corner, realizing I had a lot I would have enjoyed adding to the conversation, but could not because my own thoughts would not be welcomed.

These people were just like my friends who had abandoned me. I would be accepted only if I said the correct lines. Otherwise, I would be removed from the stage.

I firmly understood in that moment that I did not belong there. I did not belong anywhere. I went home that night and never returned to that church again.

THE RETURN

I was lonely and heartbroken. I wished my previous friends had not treated me as they had. I was frustrated that they could not understand how terribly wrong their treatment toward me had been.

Then, a revelation struck me that was enough to knock me off my feet. I had once treated someone I cared about in the exact same manner.

My ex-fiance and I had spent hours and hours chatting on the phone and restoring our friendship a few years before. But, when he revealed to me that he was not heterosexual, my acceptance of him had ended. I required him to change who he was in order to be fully embraced as my friend, something he was understandably unwilling to do. I had been wrong.

I wondered what and how he was doing now. With the help of social media, I found him and sent him a message. We began to communicate with one another, and I revealed to him that I was no longer an evangelical Christian or even a Christian at all. It felt very good to share that with someone. I had yet to tell anyone the details.

Not surprisingly, he was stunned. My refusal to compromise on any aspect of my faith had destroyed our relationship more than once. He had accepted I would always be that way, and there was nothing he could do about it.

Now, here I was describing my journey out of the faith and into a secular life. For the first time since I had left the faith, I shared my thoughts about God, life, and the world, and I was not judged. I was accepted exactly as I was. Most significantly, he offered forgiveness for the way I had treated him.

We began chatting on the phone multiple times per week and texting each other throughout the day each day. Neither of us had any interest in dating one another again, but I was thankful our friendship was restored.

I was laughing again. I was enjoying myself again. When something humorous happened, I finally had someone I could tell about it. We played video games online together with our phones on speaker phone. Even though we were geographically distant from one another, modern technology had allowed me to feel much closer to him.

My friendship with him was my salvation, for lack of a

better word, during that dark and difficult time of my life. I was no longer alone. He had forgiven me for my previous rejection and opened his heart to me once again. It was exactly what I needed.

It was enough to allow me to accept myself and my life just as it was.

ACCEPTANCE

I had no idea whether I would ever make any other friends in the future. But, I came to accept that living a life of authenticity, even if it was lived mostly alone, was preferable to living a life in which I had to deny my true self in order to socialize with others.

I had spent years denying my true desires. I had denied them so thoroughly, in fact, I wasn't even entirely aware that they were even there. My love for science, for example, had remained with me all those years. I had completely forgotten about it, yet the pain and emptiness this denial caused remained within me through it all. It did not fade until I fully embraced this aspect of myself.

WHO I AM

There is much more to myself than I ever even knew. I did not discover the combination of unique qualities that make me me until I walked away from evangelical Christianity.

The options children are exposed to in this faith are

extremely limited. Everything we think and do must have direct relevance to God. Much of my identity, therefore, was pre-determined and defined for me before I even knew what an identity was.

Now that I could explore wherever my heart led, I found many new aspects of myself that had lay dormant all those years. I had been so fearful that if I walked away from my faith, I would lose my own self. In truth, by walking away from my faith, I found myself.

I love writing. While I always knew I enjoyed writing and knew this was a talent of mine, I did not engage in writing much until after I left my faith. Every time I had sat down to write something as an evangelical Christian, it wouldn't hold my interest.

I tried writing stories with a spiritual lesson that met the stipulations of my faith, but I could never quite make it happen. I tried writing non-fiction, but it did not hold my focus.

I wanted to write about something, but I could not find anything to write about that was enjoyable and interesting to me. Nothing I tried writing about connected with me. Eventually, I stopped attempting to write.

As I worked through a time of such loneliness and social disconnection after I left my faith, I decided to give writing a try again. I was no longer bound by the rules of evangelical Christianity regarding content that was considered acceptable to write about. I could write whatever I wanted.

I experimented with blogging, and I received great enjoyment from doing so. I explored various topics through my writing and discovered what best resonates with me. Finally, I began to write a fantasy story, and when I did, I discovered a part of myself that had been deeply hidden away by my faith my entire life.

As an evangelical Christian, I would have never considered writing a story about a mystical forest containing magic, dragons, fairies, and more. Such things were considered demonic. I had never thought about this genre as an option.

Now, as I gave it a try, I found how great my love for fantasy writing actually is. Had I remained in my faith, I would have never even known.

I love music. While this was an area I was allowed to pursue in my religious upbringing, it was required to be pursued within specific guidelines. Now that I was no longer bound by these senseless rules, I discovered new genres of music that deeply connected with me.

As already noted, I love science. In particular, I love studying evolutionary biology. As a young child, I was always fascinated and even enchanted with discovering the unique characteristics of various species and how these attributes match the environment in which each species lives.

This is the core of evolutionary biology. I just didn't know it.

Of course, I was not allowed to follow this love of mine through its natural course. I was instructed to disregard science and, most of all, to disregard evolutionary theory. The one component of this world I love learning about more than anything else was taken from me at a young age. I felt so thankful that I had found my way back to it.

I wanted to be me. I was not able to be myself for many years, and I fully understood the underlying misery that comes with such a plight. I no longer lived with shame about what I love in this world. Now, I celebrated it.

I felt proud of myself. I had escaped the bonds of a religion from which many never become free. I faced the loss of almost every friend I had ever had and continued on in spite of the pain. I took the opportunity to connect with my own self and learn about who I really was. I was finally happy that I was me.

After getting to know myself much better and experiencing the joy and fulfillment that comes with living my truth, I came to understand that I am better off with a small number of friends who accept me as I am than to have a large number of friends who require me to be anyone besides myself.

MOVING ON

I continued with my studies and my two part-time jobs, all which I greatly enjoyed. I chatted with my ex-fiance and friend each day. I slowly recovered and healed from the rejection of those from my past.

My life came to mean so much more to me. If there is no afterlife, the life we are all now leading increases in value significantly. I had heard many people say that without an afterlife, life would be pointless and meaningless. After I left my faith, I could no longer grasp how such a claim could possibly be true.

Has increasing the availability of anything ever caused its value to go up? If this is the only opportunity I have to experience life, I want to savor every moment as much as I am able.

The day will come when I will be just as I once was. When the dinosaurs roamed the earth, I, as I am right now, was no where to be found. Someday, my heart will stop beating, and I will return to non-life. Much later, I will become stardust. We all will.

Knowing this, whatever I was doing on a given day, I sought joy in it. I cherished each day more than I ever had before. I found my new groove. The lingering effects of my prior faith slowly faded as time passed.

My social skills improved. My sense of humor grew tremendously. Jokes I had previously not even understood were now hilarious to me. I laughed a lot more than I previously had.

People began to talk with me more and socialize with me. I became more comfortable around other people and able to connect with them. I started to go out to eat with people from work or school. We went to the movies. We attended parties. I had them over for dinner.

Life got better. The day of my graduation came. I had worked very hard to make that day a reality. I had made my way through advanced biology courses, completed an honors thesis, and more. Most importantly, I had studied what I had chosen to study. I had pursued my own interests as I moved toward that day.

I had a degree from an accredited institution. I could now get a master's degree or a full-time job, whichever I wanted to pursue. My life was mine and no one else's.

I continued working on the research team at my university. I taught science classes to elementary-aged students, which allowed me to share my passion for scientific inquiry with the children who attended. Eventually, I began working with troubled youth affected by trauma.

My friendships deepened. While I only had a few strong friendships, that was enough for me. I was no longer lonely. I was pursuing a career that I loved. I was happy. I was myself in every way I could be.

REVEALING MY PAST

A few years passed. I was working, hanging out with my

friends, doing some volunteer work in a homeless shelter for women and children who had recently fled domestic violence, and living my life. I rarely thought about evangelical Christianity and the more painful parts of my past. I had moved on, mostly. I had learned to live for today.

I began to wonder, however, if my friends ever noticed that whenever they spoke of their past, telling stories from their adolescence or young adulthood, I never shared similar stories from my own past.

The wounds had been too fresh and raw for me to share from where I had come. For a long time, it was very painful to talk about. I only talked about it with my ex-fiance. He was the only person I knew who somewhat understood what I had been through and how it had impacted me.

When I wanted to talk about a rather embarrassing belief I once held, he helped me laugh about it and approach it more light heartedly. Over time, my wounds began to heal.

I decided I was ready to let my friends know a little about my past. I was not yet ready to discuss the full details. But, I was ready for them to know the overall story. I asked them if they would watch a movie that was of great importance to me and relevant to my past.

They agreed to do so. We sat together in a friend's living room and watched the movie, Jesus Camp. This documentary came out in 2006, and it follows a group of children who were being raised in evangelical Christian homes and attending a summer camp similar to the camp I had attended as a young person.

My friends sat in shock and dismay. Some could not sit through the entire documentary as it was too difficult to even observe. The obvious brainwashing of these children was sickening and disgusting to them.

When it was over, I told them none of what they had seen was an exaggeration. It was an accurate account of the methods evangelical Christian churches use, particularly pentecostal churches, to control and manipulate children from a young age.

I then informed them that the reason I knew this film was not an exaggeration was because I was raised in a Pentecostal church just like that documentary showed, and I had attended a camp that was basically the same as what they had just witnessed. I did not share all of the details, but I did explain that I was raised in that kind of environment and had chosen to leave as a young adult.

They were shocked. I explained it was difficult and painful to talk about, and I had not yet been ready to bring it up. But, now, I was ready, and I wanted them to know. I had always sat quietly during conversations about our childhood, etc., and I told them I wanted to be able to stop doing so.

I experienced no judgment. They responded only with support and empathy. They understood that I was a victim of these practices and assured me they were proud of me for finding my way out. With tears filling my eyes, I described to them how difficult it had been when I left the faith and lost the friendships I had had for many years.

I explained why it was so difficult to make new friends and how lonely I had been before I met them. I shared that I had been afraid to reveal any of this because I feared being laughed at or ridiculed.

They cried and lamented with me as I exposed my pain. It was an evening of great healing for me. Unlike those who had abandoned me, these true friends accepted me fully just as I am. My friends were true friends.

I no longer had to keep this part of me secret and hidden. While I refused to let it define my identity, I accepted that my past is a part of me. I was now ready to embrace it for what it was.

At our next get together, things were back to normal. We

played cornhole, drank beer, grilled food, and laughed together all evening. I was accepted. I had found my place in this world. I found where I fit.

I was me. I was who I wanted to be. No one had chosen for me. I had chosen for myself. I was finally at peace.

I went home and stood in front of my dresser in my bedroom. All those years, I had hung on to that knick knack of a high-heeled shoe, given to me at the minister's event by the woman who had told all of us that our steps are ordered of God. I had found hope and comfort at the time in her words. Now, I knew I had simply been duped.

The God of the Bible was not and is not ordering my steps. Even if he was, hypothetically, I understood there would be no reason to find comfort or hope in that reality.

I stood before my dresser and observed that high-heeled shoe and considered that it represented a part of my life that I do not wish to celebrate or cherish. I picked up the knick knack, carried it to the kitchen, and dropped it in the trash can, the same place I threw all the other refuse that had no reason to remain in my life.

My life was my own. It was no one else's, and it would never be anyone else's ever again. I ordered my own steps. I was free.

TODAY

I still live in the same city where I attended college my second time around. I have a 5-year-old son who brings me unspeakable joy. He was born out of wedlock, which is just fine with me. He experienced tremendous medical complications during the first year following his birth that have now mostly resolved.

When he was at his worst, medically, and I legitimately and with good reason feared he would not survive, I heard that many of my evangelical Christian former friends learned of my son's situation. Some stated that his condition was the result of God visiting my sins onto him, both for my leaving the church and for becoming pregnant outside of marriage.

I chose to keep quiet and not respond to such a ridiculous claim. I did not want them taking away a single moment of my time from my son. I faithfully sat by his bedside for many months until he recovered and came home.

When he was born, I had to leave my job working with troubled youth, which saddened me. I am now an author, writing under various pen names, depending on the genre. I have written fantasy, horror, non-fiction, and illustrated children's books. I am far from rich and famous, but I love what I do.

I see much of myself in my young son. He, too, loves learning about different animals and the places in which they live. I still own the animal encyclopedias my mother obtained week by week from the grocery store when I was very young. He sits for long periods, looking through them just as I once did.

We often observe various species through walks in the woods or through nature videos on YouTube, and he is always delighted when we do so. I do not know whether he will retain this interest throughout his life, but I am enjoying every minute of it while I can.

He loves stories. He loves books. He especially loves music. At the age of three, he happily sat through a 2-hour orchestra concert, fully engrossed in the performance from start to finish.

I do not have the expectation of an afterlife, so I do not believe I will have an eternity with my son. I hope that after I die, I discover I was incorrect and that we will indeed spend an eternity together, but for now, I am going with what I know.

I am a better mother because of this. I want to enjoy my son as much as possible while I have the chance. I want him to spend plenty of quality time with me so someday, when I am gone, he will have plenty to remember and cherish. That is all that he will have left of me.

We spend more time at the park. I talk to him more. We go to museums. We play games. I am intentional about the quality of my time with him. I want to have as much of him as I can while I can and vice versa.

My father was diagnosed with dementia before I left my faith. By the time I had turned from it completely, my dad no longer remembered who I was. He has since passed away.

I am unsure how he would have responded to me leaving the faith. He would have been angry, probably more with the supposedly evil universities than with me. Outside of that, I am unsure what he would have said or done.

My mother is very disappointed with me. She has asked me several times to return to the ministry. She does not understand, and likely will never understand, that such an event will never happen.

She once told me I should not have any more children. She explained that since I will not teach my children to serve Jesus, their souls will be damned to hell. According to her logic, it would be better, in that case, for the soul to never be created in the first place.

She is not able to grasp how difficult it is for me to hear that my mother believes I should not have children because children raised by me will burn in hell forever due to the way I have raised them. She cannot comprehend that she told me children are better off not being born at all than to be born to me.

My mother prays for me regularly. She prays that I will

come to see the truth once again. Her dream is for all of us to be together again someday in heaven. She fears I am ruining her chance of having her immediate family all together for eternity.

I hate that I have made my mother feel this way. However, I will not live a lie simply because my parents chose a religion and a life for me without giving me the opportunity to choose for myself. I wish I could convince my mother that I and my son will not spend eternity in hell, but I know such a goal is not reachable.

In some ways, I despise fundamentalist religions for causing these issues. However, I do not dwell on it. I do not desire to live my life in anger. There are more enjoyable aspects of life to experience, and I focus on those aspects.

Meanwhile, I have found myself to be quite comfy and toasty in a local Unitarian Universalist church. It provides a spiritual community I enjoy without requiring me to believe any creeds or statements of faith that I don't agree with.

I am accepted as an atheist there, and no one attempts to change my mind. In fact, I am not the only atheist in the congregation. The sermons are not emotionally driven like those I knew growing up. They are informative and knowledgeable. I learn from them. They help me grow and become a better person.

I initially shared nothing about my past with members of my church. I was not yet ready. However, when I joined a small group to complete the classes required for church membership, I opened up and shared a little bit of my story. Once again, I was responded to with welcome and support.

As time passed, I shared bits and pieces with those I knew and cared for. However, I had not yet openly shared all of the nitty gritty details with anyone. I did not believe I ever would or could.

If I did share it all, I believed no one would understand,

so I saw no reason to bother. Even those who tried to do so to the best of their ability would never truly understand. There was no one out there like me, and that was the way that it was.

I believed that to be true for many years. I only recently came to understand how very wrong that assumption was.

WHY I WROTE THIS BOOK

several more years passed. I was not lonely. However, in
a certain sense, I did feel all alone. I was sure there was
not anyone out there who was like me. I knew there were
evangelical Christians who had left the faith and become
atheists. However, I believed no one who was as deep into
the faith as I was had ever left it and become an atheist.

It was a bit of an isolating feeling. Friends tried to understand what I had experienced and sincerely desired to do so,
but one must truly walk the path to fully grasp it. Even my
ex-fiance, as understanding as he was, had not been raised in
the faith from a young age. Thus, while he understood more
than others due to his own experience in the church, he did
not comprehend the full experience of being born into and
raised within it.

I continued on believing that I was the only person
within my category, an evangelical Christian minister who
became an atheist. I thought I was the only one who could
genuinely understand my journey. I felt somewhat isolated.

Then, one day, I was searching for something on
YouTube, and I happened upon a video titled, "Dan Barker -

How an Evangelical Preacher became one of America's Leading Atheists."

I was so jarred by seeing this title, I cannot even remember what it was that I was initially searching for on YouTube. I played the video and listened to Dan Barker tell his story. I sat on the couch completely taken in by his story as he shared that he had been an evangelical Christian from a young age, and he had been a minister for 15 years, much longer than I had been.

Over time, he came to see that his religion was untrue. He bravely and courageously wrote a letter to his friends and family to inform them that he had become an atheist and would no longer be in ministry. He accepted the consequences of this action, whatever they may be.

Today, Dan and his wife are the co-presidents of the Freedom from Religion Foundation, and he has written multiple books, sharing what he has gleaned from his experiences. I listened more and eventually learned about The Clergy Project, an organization designed to help individuals currently in ministry who have turned from the faith and want out.

I was struck by two revelations. First, I realized how fortunate I was that I was already out of the ministry when I left the faith. I already had a career path set out for myself. While I had initially planned to become a Christian counselor after completing my studies, it was simple enough to disregard that path and choose another to which my studies applied.

How terrible it must be to come to understand one's religion is untrue while depending on a paycheck by that religion to prevent an economic catastrophe. These people not only face the risk of losing their friends and loved ones, but their livelihoods as well.

The Clergy Project is there to help these individuals form

an exit strategy and receive emotional and social support during such a significant transition. They receive this help, advice, and support from people who have experienced the same.

All of this information helped me realize something else. There were people out there who were like me. All those years, I had thought I was the only person who had experienced such a transformation. Now, I knew I wasn't.

For two days, I could not stop listening to videos of Dan Barker speaking at various engagements. I had videos on in the background as I washed dishes, mopped the floor, and drove around running errands.

I understood his words and experiences on a very deep level and knew if he were ever to talk with me, he would truly understand mine as well. It were as though for the first time, I was hearing someone who could speak my language. That sense of connection changed so much for me.

The world suddenly felt like a much less lonely place to live. I was not the only one who had walked this path.

I began to search some more. I did not know any atheists personally and had never really sought any out. I had never thought about doing so before. I had assumed I would not fit well with them given my background.

I then came across a man named Seth Andrews. He runs a website and podcast titled, "The Thinking Atheist." I found him on YouTube as he shared his story, "From Religion to Reason."

Seth had not been in ministry, but he had been raised in a home very similar to mine, and he had gone into Christian broadcasting as a young adult. He, too, eventually came to see that his religion did not make rational sense. For two more days, I then listened to him through speaking engagements via YouTube.

After that, I found even more people who had been

deeply involved in evangelical Christianity, including former ministers, who had now become atheists. Listening to these people brought a final wave of healing to my heart. That feeling of isolation vanished. There were people out there like me.

Understanding how much their stories had meant to me, I began to wonder, "Why have I never wrote about this?"

I asked myself this question even though I knew the answer. It had simply been too painful for me to talk about. For a long time, it was not something I wanted to delve into with much detail. However, now, I felt I was ready. I was ready to share what happened to me.

I was victimized by a fundamentalist religion, and I almost lost my own self as a result. However, I found my way out of that religion and to my true, authentic self. For that, I feel both very fortunate and very grateful.

Most of the people I grew up with are still deep in the faith. They never found their way out. I wonder what secrets they hold. What doubts do they push out of their minds? I will likely never know.

I wrote this book for three reasons. First, I am ready to share my story. Writing is a means through which I process and work through difficult experiences. Writing about this journey has been very beneficial for me, mentally and emotionally.

Secondly, many people who are atheists, whether they were once religious or not, seem to be interested in learning what triggered someone's ability to leave his/her faith. I think many people will simply receive enjoyment from hearing my story.

I hope it will help others outside of this faith to better understand why it is so difficult for those raised in evangelical Christianity to recognize the irrationality of their beliefs, let alone accept it. I also hope it communicates how frightening the proposition of abandoning one's faith is to the average evangelical Christian. Escaping the clutches of fundamentalist religion is extremely challenging.

Third, I wrote this book for anyone out there who is in the place in which I once found myself. This book is written for anyone who is locked into a faith that is squelching his/her true, authentic self and starting to question whether what he/she has been taught is true.

I did my best to keep the scientific information accessible to beginners and in easy to understand, lay terms. I aspire to bring individuals in this situation hope. I rejected my faith, and I survived the journey that followed.

While many parts of this path were very painful, I am happy. I am alright. You will be, too. There may not be life after death, but there is most certainly life after faith. It may not be the perfect paradise promised to you by those preaching about heaven, but it is good and wonderful. Most importantly, it is real.

Perhaps you are reading this book and considering that if you take the step you are drawn to, you will likely lose friendships with people you love. You very well may be right. And yes, it will hurt. But, you will be okay.

There is another side to this life, and it is so wonderful. I hope this telling of my story has helped you step over and see the world from where I am standing even if only for a moment, for it is absolutely beautiful.

You are not dirty. You are not filthy. You are not depraved or evil. There is goodness in you, and it is not because a supreme being brought it with him upon moving into your heart. The goodness within you is part of you. It is part of who you are. You can feel good about yourself, not because there is a God out there who loves you, but because you are indeed good.

You need not be ashamed of the questions you have been

asking about your faith. Asking questions is good. It is how we learn.

Faith is not a virtue. Kindness is a virtue. Compassion is a virtue. Fairness is a virtue. They are virtues because they make the world a better place to live when they are practiced. Faith does not do so. Doubting is good. It is good to expect evidence when someone makes a significant claim about the world or about you.

I believe I am not able to say it better than the words shared by Seth Andrews (thethinkingatheist.com) in his talk about the ultimate question, which can be found on YouTube (www.youtube.com/watch?v=csxLnEUNNS8). I listened to these words not long ago, and I was pushed to tears.

I know others have often talked of me as though I am a cautionary tale, a warning to others to be careful, or they will end up like me. I am seen as defective and someone who fell short of what could have and should have been.

But, I am none of those things. Neither are you. It felt good to hear it, and I'd like to share some of Seth's words with you now.

"You learn a lot about people when you declare that you're not gonna live your life their way...So many voices out there today are just an echo of previous voices, a hand-me-down from a previous generation, and the generation before, and the generation before...

Everyone around them looks like them, walks like them, talks like them, everyone except for you. This was not what was expected of you...

You had two choices in your life. You could keep the peace, and you could line up with the others. Or you could walk at your own pace in your own direction for your own reasons and accept the consequences and rewards that come with being your own person. And the fallout for many of you has been significant...

These days, when they look at you, they only see what they think you should have been...Yeah, they love you, but the full package, the 100% love, the unfiltered love, well, that's gonna be kept on reserve until you straighten up...

This [religion] is a prison designed to look like a mansion, and you're not gonna live like that. You've read the books, and you've seen the history, and learned the science and realized the world is much grander than most people ever imagined. You finally found your own voice, and you're going to speak in it.

You've had the epiphany that you don't owe it to the rest of the world to keep them happy...

You are not a sheep to be led, an echo to be repeated, a cautionary tale, a bad example, a freak, a pervert, shameful, broken, ugly...you are not ugly. You're beautiful.

You figured out what so many billions, literally billions, of other people have missed...

You stepped out of the crowd to stand forward, to stand out, and to stand your ground...even though you don't believe your father is a divine king who does magic...you've discovered that your life is wonderful and amazing and so much more satisfying.

It's a life where every day brings a new opportunity to ask the ultimate question. Now, is that kind of life easy?...Probably not. But, be encouraged, my friends. Because inside this 13.7 billion-year-old universe, there has never, ever been anyone exactly like you, and there never will be again. And you are simply living a unique life that reflects that fact.

And while others laugh at you because you are different, you can laugh at them because they are all the same."

If you are doubting your faith, there is not something wrong with you. This is not a weakness of yours rearing its ugly head. You are not defective. You are not falling short.

You are intelligent and rational, and that part of you, a part of you which is wonderful and good, is sorting through all of this. And that is okay.

You are unique, not only in this world, but in the entire cosmos. Don't allow a fantasy-based religion to squelch who you really are. Don't miss this one, singular opportunity to be yourself.

Embrace the doubts. Embrace reason. Embrace rational thinking, and prepare to discover your authentic self. Get out of the prison dressed up like a mansion. You will be okay. You will be free.

REFLECTIONS ON MY LIFE

A lot of people ask whether I am angry about the way fundamentalist religion affected my life. Yes, I am angry. However, I do not dwell on it. It happened, and I can either spend my life feeling unpleasant feelings about it or move on so I can enjoy the life I have left.

There are times when I think about it more, and the anger bubbles up from within. Every day of my life is precious to me, and I spent so many of them being suffocated by dogma. How much happier I could have been back then if fundamentalism had never touched my life.

When I think about this, I allow myself to feel those emotions and then, I remind myself of how fortunate I am. The reality is that most people my age who grew up in evangelical Christianity or other fundamentalist religions never found their way out. But, I did. I am one of the lucky ones. When I ponder on that, I feel better again.

I am not at all angry with my parents for raising me in this religion. They were unknowing victims as well. They both needed therapeutic interventions to help them with their very difficult problems, but such interventions were not well available when they were young.

Rich, television evangelists swooped in and exploited their vulnerability. When treatments that would have helped them did become available, it was too late. My parents had already been duped by these wicked people and pushed to turn away from mental health therapies, so they never considered them an option.

It would be easy to judge, but I grew up in a time when receiving therapy and taking medication for anxiety or depression is more socially acceptable and available. Their circumstances were different.

My mother had difficulty showing affection to me due to the paralysis of her emotions caused by her wounds. After all these years, religion has done nothing to bring her healing. That is not to say that she was a terrible mother for she most certainly was not.

I simply wish for her own sake that she had been able to receive the help she needed to process her traumatic experiences and find healing so she could move on with her life. Instead, the instructions given to her have been to pretend the pain is not there and to pray, listen to worship music, or think about God. This has affected her ability to maintain healthy friendships with her peers. I wish things were different for her. She deserved better.

Now that my dad has passed away, I feel tremendous pain when I think about the suffering he endured so consistently for so many years. I often wish he had never listened to a single television evangelist. However, I am then reminded that prior to that, my dad used alcohol as a form of anxiety medication. He easily could have become an alcoholic.

Maybe he still would have been a good father even if he had continued drinking in this manner, but I will never know. Perhaps if my dad had not found religion, he would have been a terrible father, consumed with drunkenness. On the other hand, maybe he would have been more receptive to new medications as they came out had he not found religion, and if so, maybe he would have had a much better life. Not knowing which direction things would have gone for him, it is difficult to know how to feel about it all.

I simply know that I wish my parents had experienced a more joyful life based in reality. They were good parents.

I do still miss my friends who walked away from me when I left this faith. However, hypothetically, were they to offer friendship to me once again, I do not believe I would accept the offer. I would wish them well and end it there.

I have friends today who accept me exactly as I am. They do not insist I change the core components of who I am in order to please them. My friendships today are much more deep and meaningful as a result.

After my son's extremely premature birth, while the evangelical Christians I once associated with discussed the curse of God upon my child, my friends of today came to the hospital with special gifts picked out just for me to extend comfort in whatever way they could.

They brought clothes for the baby and my favorite beverage and snacks for me. They visited and supported me. I could never go back to the way things once were with my former religion and those relationships.

I have reconnected with one friend from my former life. You may recall the story I told in which I visited the mall as a teenager with two friends of mine from church. We witnessed a fellow student who was openly a lesbian and was walking across the parking lot with another girl.

We reacted with sounds of disgust and mocked her from across the parking lot. Unbeknownst to me, one of the friends with me behaving this way was, herself, a lesbian. Not only did I not know, she did not know it, either.

A few years ago, I visited her and her wife. I mentioned this incident to her as I had worried that she had inwardly felt tormented by our actions. I was pleased to learn she had no memory of the incident, and therefore, it had not affected her so.

She went on to explain that she did not realize she was a lesbian until she fell in love with the woman who is now her wife. Prior to that, she had experienced some failed relationships with men, not really understanding why they never quite connected.

The dogma she and I were raised in had suffocated her true self so thoroughly, she was not even aware of her own sexual preferences and attractions. Years later, she was fortunate enough to meet the woman who would become her wife, and they are quite happy with a young son and now, a set of twins on the way.

How much would my friend have missed out on had she not broken free from the bigoted upbringing we both experienced? Recently, I was in her area, and we spent an evening together as my son played with their son, and we visited with one another.

One child born to two lesbians and one child born out of wedlock played with one another. Two families who are happy and filled with love spent time together. Yet, the majority of people from our past would have sneered at all of us because we fail to meet their meaningless and pointless standards.

No, I could never accept the friendship of such people moving forward unless they, like us, have rejected their former faith and turned from their bigoted ways. I can never go back to the way things were.

Some have asked me whether I at least turn to the Bible as a source of moral guidance, removing the bad parts and sticking with the good. No, I do no such thing. I have not touched a Bible in years. I no longer own a Bible nor will I ever. It would serve me no use.

First of all, how could I possibly trust the moral guidance of a book which openly condones slavery, rape, and genocide? Finding good nuggets of morality in there would be much like swimming through a feces-laden swamp in search of a Clorox® wipe deep under the filthy water. Once I find it, what good will it do for me at that point? I can think of more pleasant places to seek moral guidance.

Secondly, in order to know how to decipher the good parts from the bad parts of the Bible, one would already have to know the difference between what is moral and what is immoral before picking up the book. Otherwise, how would one know which parts are good and which parts are bad? And if one already knows such information, what guidance is there to be sought from the Bible in the first place?

Even if I were to disregard the more obviously immoral components of this book, I question even the less shocking and appalling components. In the Bible, we are instructed to love our enemies (ironically, this instruction comes from a God who damns all of his enemies to burn in hell for all eternity).

I don't love my enemies. Why would I?

We are instructed to forgive a person 490 times, consecutively. I guess 491 is the magical number after which forgiveness is no longer required. How many times would I forgive someone? Well, that depends.

When I worked with troubled youth, I sometimes felt I was offering forgiveness 490 times to the same person. However, in such cases, I understood many of their actions were rooted in mental illness which was outside of their control. If they felt sincere regret and apologized, I openly and easily forgave.

However, if someone in a right and rational mind

premeditatedly caused me harm, I'm not sure I would forgive that person even one time. Fundamentalism requires hard and fast, black and white rules, but life is more complex than this. Morality is more complex than this. We have to work all of this out rather than simply following a preset list of rules.

Perhaps you are wondering where I do find my moral guidance. I find it within myself. I understand how valuable life is. As far as we know, it is the most rare form of existence in this universe. The rest of the universe exists without even knowing that it does. We have the privilege to actually experience it consciously for a brief period of time.

Knowing this, I want to help others enjoy such an experience as much as possible. I would certainly not want to cause pain or add to someone's existing pain. I cannot solve all of the problems of the world, but I can indeed focus on my small area of the world and help those I come into contact with in whichever way I am able.

To me, morality is as simple as that. While discussions of moral dilemmas can be invigorating, the reality is that for most of us, a much more simplistic form of morality suffices for daily life. See people as valuable because they are rare and unique. Everything else regarding how to treat others will usually fall in line from there.

I do not require religion to understand how to treat other people. I do not require the promise of eternal reward or punishment to motivate me to act toward others with care. Religion actually pushed me to do the complete opposite.

Religion caused me to look down on others who were not like me. Religion led me to be bigoted even toward my own friends. Religion pushed me to pressure others into denying their authentic selves for the sake of dogma, which only decreased the happiness all of us could experience.

I accept that I cannot change the past. It happened, and I understand how it happened. I understand that the best action I could take now is to learn from all that happened and use that knowledge to better myself, my life, and my little corner of the world.

Most significantly, I believe one of the most appropriate ways I can impact the world is to be a good mother to my son. It is only natural to prioritize our own offspring.

I will teach my son how to be a critical thinker, but I will never instruct him regarding what to believe. I only want him to know how to evaluate claims to determine their veracity.

People have asked whether I would accept my son choosing a specific religion. Of course I would. I do believe the chances of him turning to a fundamentalist religion are quite low, however, since I will insure he knows how to think critically. Critical thinking and dogma do not mix well.

I want him to have the freedom to pursue that which connects and resonates with him, whatever that may be. I know what it is like to not have that opportunity, and I understand how important it is to never deny him that.

I am not thankful that I endured those years in evangelical Christianity, but I am thankful for the lessons I gained from them. I hold a great appreciation for the freedom I now have. It is a freedom many take for granted, but I never will. I get to be myself. I get to enjoy being myself. I remember this each and every day. There are many out there who do not have such a privilege.

If I were allowed a wish that impacted only myself and my family, I would wish that my parents received the therapeutic interventions they needed at the time they needed them. My parents would have had the opportunity to live much happier and more fulfilling lives.

I would make that wish for their own sake, but I would also wish it for my own. Had my parents received the help they needed, they would not have been so vulnerable to the manipulative practices of television evangelists. My upbringing would not have been so limiting, and I could have experienced more happiness and fulfillment earlier on.

But, there is no means through which such wishes can ever come true. There is no time machine. There is no magic. It cannot be changed.

I am happy and fulfilled now. Knowing what a difference it makes to be so, I do what I can to help others be happy and fulfilled as well. I am free, and my life is mine and mine alone. I hope you will spend your days insuring you can say the same.

REFLECTIONS ON HUMANITY

Why do so many people believe in God? I have both
asked this question and been asked this question by
others on numerous occasions. Some believe the very fact
that we have a tendency to believe in God is proof of the
existence of God. As you can guess by now, I disagree with
this conclusion.

We are fortunate to have the facility to reflect on our own
species and how and why we came to be as we are. We very
well may be the first species in the entire universe able to do
such a thing even if life does exist elsewhere.

We are pattern seekers. Much of our intelligence evolved
around the ability to determine cause and effect. This helped
our survival. We also tend to accept information given to us
by someone we view as an authority. It is in our nature.

In a world wrought with dangers around every turn,
these pattern seeking and authority accepting behaviors
served us well. Identifying cause and effect relationships and
gaining information from those older and wiser than us was
quite beneficial. Thus, nature selected for these tendencies in
our species.

However, consider the explanation I gave about our spines. It provided us with an advantage to stand upright, yes. But, there was a compromise. The system is not perfect. Along with this adaptation, we also became prone to incurring back injuries. Upright walking was more advantageous than a tendency to back injuries was disadvantageous, so we developed upright walking in spite of this accompanying defect.

Likewise, our pattern seeking behavior was advantageous to our survival, but it brought along problems of its own. We have a difficult time recognizing when a pattern does not actually exist. We find patterns where they are not.

When we conduct scientific studies, we have to take great care to insure human bias does not affect the data because we are so prone to error when evaluating whether a pattern is present or absent. This defect of ours is specifically why we must follow the scientific method so carefully and submit data to statistical analyses.

We are not nearly as bright as we think we are. Just as our backs are prone to injury, our evaluation of cause and effect is prone to error. It is in our nature to see patterns in everything. The concept of random occurrences without reason are difficult and, in some cases, impossible for us to fully grasp. We want known causes to satisfy our yearning for patterns.

So, when water routinely fell from the sky and loud thunder roared, we wanted a cause to explain it. Not having the technology to understand what rain and thunder actually is, we made up the cause that we needed. All we could think of was that a god was doing it because a ridiculous cause was preferred to no cause at all.

Our pattern seeking behavior led to the invention of God. From there, the idea of God continued because we also have the tendency to accept the instruction and teachings of authority, another aspect of ourselves that is both a blessing and a curse.

When prehistoric mommy knew a plant was poisonous, she informed little prehistoric Johnny that that plant is poisonous and he will die if he eats it. Little Johnny had authority-accepting genes, accepted that as true, and survived to pass on his authority-accepting genes. The little prehistoric Johnnys that lacked such genes were more likely to eat the plant when mommy wasn't looking, subsequently die, and take their genes with them to the grave.

The authority-accepting genes won out. So, when prehistoric mommy and daddy decided God made it rain, they taught that information to little prehistoric Johnny who had authority-accepting genes. Johnny accepted this as true and passed this information on to his children along with his authority-accepting genes and so on and so forth.

This is why a belief in God began and why a belief in God has continued. Different groups selected different gods, which is why literally thousands of gods have been invented by humans throughout our existence.

Yet, so many believe that the one god they were raised to serve is the one, true god out of all of the thousands that have been invented by our species. As Christopher Hitchens often said before he passed away, people used to believe in hundreds or thousands of gods. Then, they believed in only a few. Now, most believe in only one. They are getting closer and closer to the actual figure as time goes on.

We continue to do as our species has done for millennia and seek patterns, filling the gaps in our knowledge with God. We have an inherent need to identify and understand the cause of anything we observe. This is the only need God has ever truly fulfilled for us.

WHAT'S THE HARM?

So, we understand why we tend to believe in God. It's an error of our nature. Does it matter? Why not just go on believing in God then?

If a belief in God was causing no harm to anyone, I would say, most certainly, carry on and enjoy. As you have seen from my story, though, our tendency to believe in God certainly caused me harm. But, the harm caused to me is quite mild compared to the suffering others have endured at the hands of people who believed they were pleasing a supreme being floating around in the sky.

People have been burned alive. People had their hearts removed from their chests to supposedly insure God would cause the sun to rise the next day. Wars have broken out over differing beliefs about God. Suicide bombers are rarely atheists.

But, that sort of harm is obvious. There are other types of harm that are much more subtle, and this more subtle harm may very well cause the destruction of our species.

We are a tribal species. We evolved in small groups who lived cooperatively with one another, sharing and working together. This is why we receive a burst of pleasure when we help someone. And this is a wonderful aspect of our species.

Some believe evolutionary theory requires that we be entirely selfish beings, caring only of our own welfare. There are indeed species who live this way. But, we are a social species (and we are not the only one). The early individuals of our species survived more frequently if they tended to work cooperatively in a group. Those who were loners and preferred to manage on their own did not fare as well.

We evolved to live within tribes because this was advantageous to our survival. We desire community. We long to be with others who are similar to ourselves, and we care about people we consider to be in our group.

However, we also evolved in an environment in which we competed with other tribes for limited resources. For this reason, we also have the tendency to feel wary of and uncaring toward those who are outsiders. When people are considered to be "others," that care and compassion easily ends.

The human species has certainly committed terrible atrocities, no one can deny this truth. There is, indeed, a dark side to our species, and it can be found within this tendency of ours. We innately hold prejudice against those different from us, and this has caused many a great scourge throughout our history.

There was once a reason for this attribute that served us well. As hunter-gatherer tribes, we had good reason to be wary of members of competing tribes. We had to look out for our own tribe and no one else as we competed for resources in a harsh environment. Thus, genes that led us to behave this way were selected for by nature.

In today's modern world, such wariness serves no purpose and is futile, though. We do not live in tribes who are competing for resources. We are not hunter-gatherers anymore. Everything is different now. Yet, we still tend to behave with an "us versus them" mentality because this behavior is in our genetic code.

Racism, homophobia, and other such issues plague our society. We have proven that we are quick to drop bombs on other nations, killing masses of innocent people, for we do not see them as part of "us." They are not in our tribe.

We also see this us versus them mentality within religions. Religion, especially fundamentalist religion, provides us with community. It provides a tribe. It also causes us to see everyone else who is of a different faith or no faith at all as "them."

We don't care much for people that we consider to be "them." When Christopher Hitchens, a famous author and atheist, was diagnosed with terminal cancer years ago, the internet was flooded with comments of glee and celebration from many evangelical Christians. Many expressed joy at the thought of him standing before God, realizing he was wrong, and then, being filled with regret as he is cast into a lake of fire for all eternity.

How could anyone possibly wish something so terrible onto another human being for no other reason than disagreeing with his/her belief? I ask that question even though I know the answer. To those people, Christopher Hitchens was one of "them." He was an outsider. He was not a member of the tribe. So, the possibility of care and compassion dissolved.

I myself had once been an "us" in the evangelical Christian church. However, as soon as I became a "them," care and compassion for me ended abruptly. That care and compassion became so absent that some of these people who had once called themselves my friends experienced happiness upon hearing of my son's medical emergency and tragedy. Because he was my son, he was a "them," too.

Besides the obvious suffering such terrible acts cause on individuals, this tendency of ours to find community in religion and then, separate ourselves from one another is a danger to the existence of our species. What's the harm? That's the harm. It could cause our extinction.

We are not hunter-gatherers any longer. Most humans eat food grown on farms or created by the food industry. We live in a very different world. Our population is exploding. By the end of this century, it is expected that there will be 12 billion people living on this planet.

Resources will once again become limited. However, if we compete for them, our tools of destruction are much greater now. We will not come after one another with spears and arrows as our ancestors once did. We will use bombs, even nuclear bombs, to secure the resources we need to survive. It is unlikely in this scenario that our species will sustain itself.

But, there is a better way. We are intelligent beings, and perhaps we can find solutions to many of the world's complex problems. Maybe we can find a way to increase access to resources. Maybe we can produce more food. Maybe we can clean more water.

We could find a way to increase the chance that our species will survive. But, we cannot do that if we will not work together. Religion promotes our tribal tendencies, and these tendencies could be the very trait that destroys us.

We absolutely must work together toward a solution if we are ever to find one. But, we cannot do that if we are so hateful and loathing of others that we are fantasizing about them being cast into a lake of fire and burning for all eternity.

On top of this is the delusion religion brings that we need not worry about the survival of our species. "God created us with a special purpose, and he will make sure that purpose is fulfilled. We are why the universe exists in the first place, so he would never stand by and allow our entire species to disappear. "

What motive would a person holding such a belief have to invest efforts into securing the future of our species? That person already believes our future is secured through a magical being in the sky.

I have often heard evangelical Christians use this exact argument. Why worry about any of it when God is going to come and fix everything?

What if God is not going to come and fix everything? What if we are not a species specially selected by a divine being? What if no one is watching out for us but ourselves? All evidence says that no one else is.

Fundamentalist religions divide us. Belief in God promotes apathy toward the plight of our species. It sows seeds of doubt in the scientific process. But, these are not the only dangers.

These beliefs blind people from our true roots, which is our evolutionary history, and that matters. With all we are facing in the world today that threatens our species' very survival, our hope will not be found in God. It will be found in evolution.

MOVING FORWARD

The future of our species may look bleak. However, there is reason to be optimistic. Our hope can be found in evolution.

Genes that no longer serve any purpose eventually fade. When a trait is no longer advantageous to survival, nature no longer selects for it.

We once had to grab ahold of every resource we could, sharing only with close members of our tribe as we needed those members in order to survive. We once had to fight with nearby tribes to protect our limited resources. There was a reason these genes were selected for. That reason, however, no longer exists.

In the earlier years of our species, those who were overly trusting or comfortable with people from other tribes were much less likely to survive as they could easily lose their lives in competition for limited resources. Whatever genes they had that made them this way were not given the chance to spread as a result.

This particular genetic composition likely did appear here and there, due to random mutation, but it could never make its way further into the various populations because the person with this genetic composition was less likely to survive, reproduce, and pass on his/her genes.

But, the world is different now. While most of us are competing for jobs, promotions, and other such things, very few of us are killing others in order to secure resources for ourselves. There would be no reason for a person with this genetic composition to be less likely to survive and reproduce.

Let me give an example of an evolutionary trait fading in our species to demonstrate what I am suggesting. We are descendants of species covered with comparatively large amounts of hair. That was once advantageous to survival. However, things changed. Our ancestors became more intelligent due to natural selection, and, as a result, became able to use the fur of their prey to protect themselves from the elements.

Before that, if someone came along with a gene for less hair, that person would be less likely to survive and reproduce. Thus, every time a gene for less hair showed up, it soon disappeared. Our ancestors remained hairy.

But, once our ancestors became intelligent enough to figure out how to use the fur of animals, someone could come along with a gene for less hair and survive and reproduce just as well as those who were more hairy.

It is not that having hairy bodies then became harmful to us. Hairy bodies simply served no useful purpose any longer. So, such genes slowly disappeared, not because they were selected against, but simply because they were no longer selected for. This process takes longer for a gene to fade away, but it happens.

Today, we only have an evolutionary remnant from our hairier history. We do have hair, but not much compared to other primates who depend on their hair or fur for survival.

This gives us the hope that given time, the genes that produce traits of wariness toward those different from us will fade, leaving only a tiny remnant as a reminder of this dark component of our species' history. In fact, I believe that evolutionary change may be in the process of occurring within our species right now.

Sometime between 12,000 and 23,000 years ago, in most areas of the world, our ancestors figured out how to grow their own food. This was revolutionary for our species. While it brought many changes and possibilities to us, I want to focus on one particular change it brought about.

There was no real advantage any longer to behave in a tribal manner. Think about it. As hunter-gatherers, dependent on the food that naturally showed up in the wild, we had good reason to keep other tribes away. If we didn't, they could consume some of the food we needed, and we could starve.

But, once we figured out how to grow our own food, we could grow entire fields of food. It really would not matter if someone else we did not know was doing the same a short distance away.

When we were a hunter-gatherer species, if a gene came along that gave an individual the tendency to be friendly toward other tribes, that person would be much less likely to survive and that gene would vanish. That gene could have shown up again and again, but it could just never make it.

But, once we became an agricultural species, that changed. Someone with such a gene could come along and survive just fine. It's not that those with genes for more tribal behaviors became harmful. Nature simply no longer selected for such genes because they no longer promoted our survival.

People with a tendency to be friendly toward other tribes were now just as likely to survive as those with a tendency to be wary of other tribes. Wariness of others was no longer selected for by nature.

Of course, this does not mean that genes for tribal behaviors vanished within a few generations. This process takes a very, very long time. Our ancestors did not lose most of their hair within a few generations after learning to wear fur to keep warm. It took a long time for those genes to fade, and it will take a long time for these genes for tribal behavior to fade, too.

But, they will fade. We know this because we have learned that this is how natural selection works. When a gene is no longer selected for, it slowly disappears until it leaves nothing but a remnant.

We still have plenty of problems with racism, homophobia, and other such behaviors rooted in tribalism today. Those genes are still here with us. But, we are not as racist, homophobic, or tribalistic as we once were.

We tend to think that we are advancing in this area simply because we are learning more than those before us did. Perhaps that is correct. But, perhaps there is another explanation. Perhaps the genetic composition for the "us versus them" thinking is slowly fading from our species over thousands and thousands of generations, beginning when we became an agriculture species.

Maybe less and less of our species has inherited such genes over time because nature no longer selects for them and thus, more and more of us are open to accepting those who are different from ourselves. If this is true, the changes we need to occur so we can work together to solve the problems that threaten our species are already slowly taking place.

Over time, we very well may become less and less tribalist until that behavior is rarely seen with any significance. When that happens, we will be able to cooperate across the globe and come up with what will assuredly be brilliant ideas. But, this is all assuming our species survives long enough for that to take place as such a process takes an extremely long time.

Time could run out for us if we do not adapt quickly enough. Let it be a sobering thought that 99.9% of species that have ever been housed on this planet failed to make such an adaptation at some point quickly enough when things changed. They were then swallowed into extinction. Those that did not leave fossilized remains have had any and all possibility of memory or knowledge that they were ever here irreversibly erased.

It absolutely could happen to us. We could soon disappear, much sooner than we seem to realize. While our mark on this world would surely remain until near its end, who would be here to discover our rich history and existence? We would not only cease to exist. We would cease to be remembered.

It seems risky to leave this in the hands of genetic change. Fortunately, there is another way we can use evolution to save our species.

Evolution gave us an extraordinary gift. Our genes give us these tribal behaviors and other negative things we would do better without. But, our genes also give us the ability to reason, and because of our ability to reason, many of our genetic tendencies do not have to be our destiny.

Using my intelligence, I can admit that I respond differently, emotionally, when a person very different from me is approaching me on the street. I can also use my intelligence to consider that such feelings are based on instincts that no longer match the environment in which I live. I have the intellectual capacity to understand that today, such tendencies only increase harm if I allow them to influence my thoughts or actions.

With that understanding, I can then use reason to determine that treating this person differently or maliciously is uncalled for and damaging. I can choose to behave kindly toward this person, understanding that kindness is the behavior this person likely deserves and understanding that my innate feelings are ridiculous.

As I treat those different from me with respect and fairness and nothing terrible happens to me as a result, my brain will learn and adapt in response to these experiences. In time, those innate feelings tend to fade as a result of these changes within my brain.

We are the first species on this earth who has learned and come to understand enough about our world and our evolutionary history to be capable of overriding some of our natural instincts. While nature may push us to be one way, we are the first species on this planet with the capacity to push back and say, "No. I do not want to be that way. I won't be that way."

Let us not take such a unique, rare, and precious skill for granted. This singular skill may be the one trait that rescues us from our own impending extinction. "Us versus them" is going to destroy our species. In today's current world, kindness, care, and cooperation are what will save us. Every time we choose kindness, care, and cooperation, we contribute to the survival of our species.

Religions that claim they have found the truth, however, are not going to assist us with this process. They have and will continue to impede it. They spread the false information that evolution and the process of natural selection is not how we came to be. When those raised in such faiths believe this, like I once did, their path through reason takes them in the wrong direction.

With that incorrect information, when they feel negative emotions about someone different from them, they then reason that because God has designed us, these feelings are legitimate and helpful. Thus, they decide they should pay attention to these feelings and choose to respond accordingly.

Knowing this, it is not surprising that during the civil rights movement, fundamentalist faiths were at the forefront of the fight against racial integration in schools and society as a whole. They argued it is God's design, and they argued this because they believed those instincts they were born with were placed within them by God.

It is not surprising that as gay marriage was recently legalized, evangelical Christians have stood at the forefront of the fight against equal rights for gay people. It is not surprising that as transgender individuals stand up for their own rights, evangelical Christians are standing against them as well.

When we misunderstand who we are and how we came to be, we make grave errors in judgment. We embrace instincts that we should reject. Kindness, care, and cooperation are thrown out the window. Our species can no longer afford to do this.

Some may argue against this, pointing out missionary work that has been carried out to help people in other countries or other such charitable work. However, I have been on these mission trips. I have experienced them for myself.

While these evangelical Christians are working hard to build a school, a hospital, or whatever, they are doing so for the purpose of converting those who will use that resource to their religion. They are not simply working to alleviate the suffering of another or to work together with others to make the world a better place. They are striving to go to "them" and make them an "us." It is still divisive in intent.

Consider the treatment I received from evangelical Christians when I stopped being an "us" in their eyes. I was cut off, and my suffering did not matter to any of them. They believe that by following these tribal instincts, they are being obedient to God.

There can be no good from teaching young children that they and all other people are wicked and vile. We do not help anyone by teaching others to believe that all people are evil and depraved unless a specific God enters their hearts and brings his goodness to them. With such a view, there is the "us," consisting of goodness, and the "them," consisting of evil.

I believe better about humans as a whole. While we have our share of sociopaths and psychopaths for sure (who do not appear to be swayed from their harmful actions by the threats of hell made by the religious), most of us receive joy from helping others live a better and more fulfilling life, and we do not require the instruction of God to do it.

We only need to reflect on our tribal tendencies, understand their roots and lack of fitness in the current world, and reject them. Treat others as though they are a part of our tribe even if they are different from us. Because we receive pleasant, good feelings when we help members of our tribe, we will be happy doing exactly this and we will work toward sustaining our species at the same time. It is as simple as that.

We must educate our children in such a way that they are fully aware of their natural instincts and how such instincts came to be. We must help them understand the harm our species will endure if these traits are embraced in the current environment. The denial of evolution and natural selection will impede us from reaching this goal.

We can no longer afford these religions that blind us from reality. We must do away with them.

God is not going to save us. We must save ourselves.

I am optimistic. I do believe religions that discourage critical thinking and learning about the world are going to fade. I believe it will happen much more quickly than many of us currently realize.

The internet, I predict, is changing and will continue to change everything for us. I have considered that perhaps things could have potentially gone much differently for me were I born today even if I were raised in the same family and in the same environment. I wonder if I had had access to a service in which I could anonymously ask questions or seek out information without anyone knowing, would I have done so during those brief periods of doubt?

What would I have done if I had had access to people to whom I could ask questions without fear of judgment simply because they did not know who I was? What if I could have easily looked up articles to learn more about the answers to the questions I had? Would I have looked just enough to come across some information that would have changed the entire trajectory of my younger years?

Parents who are raising their children in these limiting environments are going to have more and more difficulty hiding the world from their children because the world is now so much more accessible. Children raised in these primitive beliefs are now able to fact check what they are told with ease. This access to information, I believe, will ultimately destroy these religions.

More and more, the coming generations are going to stop looking toward the sky for the rescue we need. Instead, they will look to their left and to their right toward one another. If we are to ever find a solution to humanity's problems, we will find it there.

If we can keep our species going long enough, the day is going to come when the faiths of today will appear as ridiculous to the average human being as the myths of the Greek gods now appear to the average person. Faith and hope will be placed in our own selves. Creativity and learning about the world will become the priority. Perhaps then, our species will be saved...at least for now.

Someday, our sun will explode. Our solar system will no longer exist. All life on earth will be gone. There will be no one who remembers that we ever were. The universe will carry on without us.

If this makes you feel sadness, you are not alone. But, a statement is not false simply because we do not find joy in it. We were all once non-life. The matter of which you and I are made existed before you and I lived as people. Once you die, that same matter will continue to exist. In this sense, you will always exist in one form or another.

You will only be conscious and aware of that existence, however, for a very brief period of time. We who are alive and aware are all here simply trying to make the best of this rare and precious gift we have been given. Knowing that, the idea of treating each other with ill-will or living only for one's self gain is rather appalling to me.

This understanding pushes me to choose kindness toward others. I often reflect on a profound and infamous quote by Carl Sagan in his book, Pale, Blue Dot, published in 1994, two years before his death. I was graduating from high school when he published this amazing book filled with both wonder and wisdom. I was too busy pursuing my faith to take notice of this incredible man, so I did not discover him or his work until many years later.

How much I could have learned from him at a young age had I been given the opportunity. I have always had a love for learning about the cosmos. I am so curious to hear and learn what is out there, perhaps due to the early experiences I had with my dad in the back yard with his telescope.

Carl Sagan's entire book, Pale, Blue Dot, was inspired by an image of our planet taken from nearly four billion miles away. In the image, the earth appears to be little more than a speck of dust suspended in darkness, surrounded by many other specks of dust.

He observed the photo and reflected on how incredibly tiny we are in the scope of the cosmos, and he wrote these words:

"Consider again that dot. That's here. That's home. That's us. On it, everyone you love, everyone you know, everyone you ever heard of, every human being who ever was lived out their lives. The aggregate of our joy and suffering, thousands of confident religions, ideologies, and economic doctrines, every hunter and forager, every hero and coward, every creator and destroyer of civilization...in the history of our species lived there on a mote of dust...

The earth is a very small stage in a vast, cosmic arena. Think of the rivers of blood spilled by all those generals and emperors so that in glory and triumph, they could become the momentary masters of a fraction of a dot...

Our posturings, our imagined self-importance, the delusion that we have some privileged position in the universe are challenged by this point of pale light. Our planet is a lonely speck in the great, enveloping, cosmic dark. In our obscurity, in all this vastness, there is no hint that help will come from elsewhere to save us from ourselves.

The earth is the only world known so far to harbor life. There is no where else, at least in the near future, to which our species could migrate...like it or not, for the moment, the earth is where we make our stand.

It has been said that astronomy is a humbling and character building experience. There is perhaps no better demonstration of the folly of human conceits than this distant image of our tiny world. To me, it underscores our responsibility to deal more kindly with one another and to preserve and cherish the pale, blue dot, the only home we've ever known."

We are all here trying to enjoy a smidgen of joy and happiness before the opportunity is gone from us forever. Let us help one another in that pursuit. Let us choose kindness.

We do not have a privileged place in this universe. The here and now is it. This life is all that you and I have. Make it a good one.

Connect with other people. Find a way to make this world a better place than it was before you arrived. Breathe the fresh air. Seek opportunities to show kindness to others. Do not rush through your days. Savor them. They are the only ones you will ever consciously experience.

The meaning of your life will not be found in the sky. You will find it within yourself. You get to define the meaning of your life. You get to design your own purpose. And that is absolutely wonderful.

Life is one the most rare and precious components of this universe. You are one of the very few chunks of matter that will ever receive such a gift. But, you will not have it for long. So, live it up, live it big, and live it all.

Your life is yours and yours alone.

FIND ME ONLINE

Visit my website at
AuthorCassieFox.com

Find me on Facebook at
https://www.facebook.com/Cassie-Fox-106149230846889

APPENDIX

MORE ABOUT NEURONS

Before we get into more depth about neurons and nerve impulses, it is important to have a basic understanding of a few concepts in chemistry. If you have never studied chemistry and feel intimidated, fear not. We are only discussing a few basic principles.

Look around you. Everything that you see is made of atoms. Indeed, even that which you do not see, such as the air, is made of atoms. If we were to look at water so closely that we could see the atoms that form it, we would find, as you probably know, $H2O$...two hydrogen atoms and one oxygen atom bound together.

When two or more atoms bind together like this, we call it a molecule. If we were to break those atoms apart, we would still have two hydrogen atoms and an oxygen atom, but we would no longer have water. We would have hydrogen and oxygen. These are elements, and we can find information about them on the periodic table of elements.

Atoms are composed of three subatomic particles: neutrons, protons, and electrons. The center, or nucleus, of an atom contains its neutrons and protons. The atom's electrons move around the nucleus. In the image below, the lines encircling the center (the nucleus) show the paths the electrons travel around the nucleus.

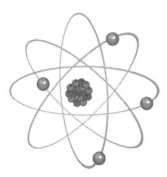

The differences between one type of atom, such as a hydrogen atom, and another type of atom, such as an oxygen atom, is the number of protons in the nucleus. Hydrogen has one proton while oxygen has eight.

Protons carry a positive charge, and electrons carry a negative charge. If an atom has the same number of protons and electrons, the atom will be neutral because the positive and negative charges of the protons and electrons each balance one another out.

But, some atoms tend to lose an electron. For example, potassium and sodium both tend to lose an electron. When they do, the atoms have one more proton than the number of electrons. The result is a positive charge. Thus, sodium and potassium atoms tend to carry a positive charge.

Similarly, if an atom gains an electron, it will have a negative charge because it has one more electron than it does protons. Atoms that carry a charge are called ions.

Before we get back to discussing neurons and nerve impulses, it is important to cover one more concept. If you were to take some sodium and dump it into a glass of water, the sodium would not just rest within the top portion of the water in a clump. That is not how atoms or molecules behave.

The sodium would spread out more and more until the concentration of sodium in the entire glass of water was equal throughout. When you first dumped the sodium into the water, you created an area in the water with a high sodium concentration. Because of the manner in which atoms and molecules behave, the sodium quickly moved from that area of higher concentration to areas of lower concentration until there was no longer a difference of concentrations in each portion of the water.

Atoms and molecules that are highly concentrated in one area of fluid will move to areas with lower concentrations of that same atom or molecule. The greater the difference in concentrations, the more rapid the movement will be.

Now that we have covered this information, we can look more closely at the action potential of a neuron. Remember that neurotransmitters released by a neighboring cell bind to receptors on the dendrites of a neuron. When enough of a neurotransmitter binds to these receptors, specific gates or doors in the top of the axon of the neuron open.

Before that event occurs, however, there is an important difference between the inside and outside area of that neuron that must be noted. The inside of a neuron contains a concentration of potassium ions that is much higher than the concentration of potassium ions outside of the neuron. Also, the concentration of sodium ions outside the cell is much greater than the concentration of sodium ions inside the cell.

So, we have a cell with a high concentration of potassium ions inside (compared to the outside) and a high concentration of sodium ions outside (compared to the inside). This difference in concentrations is called a concentration gradient.

Along the axon are doors that allow only specific substances to pass through. There are doors that only allow sodium ions through, and there are doors that only allow potassium ions through.

When the doors for sodium ions, called sodium channels, open at the top of the axon, the sodium ions rush into the cell due to the lower concentration of sodium ions inside the cell. The doors for potassium ions, called potassium channels as you would expect by now, then open, and potassium ions rush out of the cell due to the lower concentration of potassium ions outside the cell.

This rapid movement of positively charged ions across the membrane of the neuron changes the polarization in that area of the cell. This depolarization signals for the sodium channels just further down the axon to open as well, and the result is the same. Sodium ions rush in and potassium ions rush out.

This then depolarizes the next area of the axon, which then opens the sodium channels there and so on and so forth. This process continues all the way to the end of the axon until the depolarization of the cell there signals for the release of neurotransmitters into the synaptic gap. The sodium and potassium channels close, and it is over.

Now, imagine this process happening over and over again. Eventually, there will no longer be a difference between the concentration of sodium ions and potassium ions inside and outside of the cell. Everything would equalize, the concentration gradient would cease to exist, and the neuron would no longer be able to transmit messages.

One mechanism the neuron has to address this is a sodium-potassium pump. This pump transfers three sodium ions out of the cell while simultaneously transferring two potassium ions into the cell. The concentration gradient is maintained.

While this explanation goes into more depth than that which I provided elsewhere in the book, it is still only an overview of a much more complicated process. If you are fascinated by this material, I recommend reading <u>Biological Psychology</u> by James W. Kalat. While this is an expensive textbook, you can purchase an older edition for a much lower cost.

MORE ABOUT DNA

Before we talk about DNA, it is important to first talk about protein. There are many kinds of proteins, and the various types of protein serve different functions.

Picture a protein as though it were a train. Each train car, in this analogy, is an amino acid. Amino acids are the building blocks of protein. Which amino acids a protein has and the order of those amino acids determine the type of protein it is and its function.

Look over the fictional protein below and the individual amino acids from which it is formed.

Histidine - Leucine - Lysine - Phenylalanine

Of course, a protein is made of many more amino acids than this. However, using less amino acids in this example will keep the explanation more simple and easy to understand.

Imagine each of those words is a train car that, when connected, form a train. In the same way, these individual amino acids connect to one another to form a protein.

If we were to switch the order of the amino acids, moving histidine to the end and phenylalanine to the beginning, for example, we would create a different protein entirely.

Now, set that information aside just for a moment while we look at DNA. DNA is made up of four building blocks called nucleotides: adenine (A), thymine (T), guanine (G), and cytosine (C).

A DNA sequence will looking something like this:

ACG-TAC-ATG-CAG

Notice that the nucleotides are split up into groups of three. I have added the hyphens to make what I am about to explain easier to visualize, but in actual DNA, it would simply be CGATACATGCAG. The sequence of three nucleotides codes for an amino acid, which is why we often separate them into groups of three when observing a sequence of DNA. This is how DNA instructs the body to make various proteins.

So, for example, if ACG codes for histidine, and ACG is the first group of three in a DNA sequence, such as in our example above, then, histidine will be the first amino acid in the protein. If TAC codes for Leucine, Leucine will be the next amino acid. If ATG codes for Lysine and CAG codes for Phenylalanine, we can see how the above DNA sequence can code for the fictional protein described above.

Let's say this particular protein causes a person to have brown hair. That person with that DNA sequence will have brown hair because his/her DNA codes for that particular protein. These DNA sequences are stored within chromosomes.

When cells reproduce, they make identical copies of their own selves. During this process, the DNA is copied so the new cell will have the same DNA. When a gamete (a sperm or egg) is being created, however, this process goes further. That new cell splits into two. Half of the chromosomes go into one cell and the rest go into the other.

When a sperm, which contains only half of the necessary chromosomes, meets with an egg, which also contains only half of the necessary chromosomes, they combine to create one full set of chromosomes. This combination of chromosomes creates a unique individual.

Let's go back to the step in which the DNA is copied in order to reproduce a new cell. This is not a perfect process. Occasionally an error is made.

Sometimes, a pair of nucleotides are reversed. Consider our example above (ACG-TAC-ATG-CAG). Suppose this error is made with the first two nucleotides, causing the DNA sequence of the new cell to be CAG-TAC-ATG-CAG. The first set of three, which was once ACG is now CAG. Now, when that DNA codes for a protein in the new cell, instead of histidine being the first amino acid in the protein, phenylalanine will be the first amino acid instead since CAG codes for phenylalanine. It will now code for a different protein.

*Note: These particular sequences do not actually code for those specific amino acids. The proteins and sequences here are entirely fictional and only being used to describe this process, which is not fictional.

It is only a small change, but changing an amino acid in a protein can produce a significant difference. It will not be the same protein, and it will not have the same function. This can lead to a new trait being introduced into a population.

Another error that can happen is a nucleotide being missed. It is then deleted from the sequence in the new cell. This can have dramatic consequences. Imagine again our fictional DNA sequence from above (ACG-TAC-ATG-CAG).

Suppose that during the copy of this DNA sequence, the first T is omitted due to an error.

Now, we have ACG-ACA-TGC-AGG. In this case, it is not only one amino acid that is affected. All of the amino acids coded for in that sequence following the missing T are affected because all nucleotides downstream from that error will now shift up a spot, including the nucleotides further down the sequence that code for a different protein entirely.

The proteins the DNA within that chromosome codes for will be very different compared to its mother cell. A similar error can happen during which a nucleotide is added to the sequence. This offers potential for a drastic change in traits as well.

Note that these errors do not always result in a different trait. Much of our DNA is "off" or not being used. If such an error takes place in a section of DNA that is off, it will not have an effect.

Then again, a change in a DNA sequence like this can sometimes cause genes that were previous off to now be on. This is obvious how this could result in an individual with a different or even new trait.

Of course, even if this changed DNA sequence is located in a portion of genes that are on, whether this gene even shows up in the population depends on whether the gamete formed from that error is fertilized to create an individual containing that new gene.

In order for such errors in DNA copying to result in a new gene being introduced into a population, the error must be made in the formation of a gamete and the resulting gamete with the new gene must be fertilized. At this stage, it is all due to random chance.

Once that gamete is fertilized and a new individual is created as a result, natural selection takes over and determines whether that new gene will spread or disappear over time. Natural selection, as we have seen, is not at all random. This is how genetic mutations occur and result in a population containing variation.

There is much more to learn about this process that was not covered here. If you would like to learn more, please see the Additional Reading section in this appendix.

MORE ABOUT EVOLUTION

In chapter seven, I explained that individuals in a population can break off from their original population and form a new one in a new location. I described how the new environment and its differing selection pressures can cause the genetic make-up of a population to change. That is actually not the only force that could potentially be at work in this scenario.

GENOTYPES AND ALLELES

Before we continue, it is important to explain a little about genetics. For any gene you have, you have two alleles that form that gene, one from each parent. Alleles are two alternate forms of a gene.

Remember in the section, "More about DNA," I listed a fictional DNA sequence. That sequence would be considered an allele, one form of a gene. An allele with a different DNA sequence would exist right along side it. An allele can be dominant or recessive.

Together, the two alleles, or forms of the gene, from each parent join to create the individual's genotype. This genotype determines that individual's phenotype, which means the physical traits the individual has as a result of his/her genotype.

Let us consider eye color. My parents both have brown eyes, but my eyes are blue. How did that happen?

It happened because both of my parents' genotypes for eye color are Bb. B, which codes for brown eyes, is one allele and b, which codes for blue eyes, is another allele. Only one allele is passed on to offspring from each individual, so an individual with genotype Bb will pass on either the B or the b.

In this case, B is the dominant allele and b is the recessive allele. Anyone who has B will have the phenotype brown eyes regardless of the other allele. BB and Bb will both result in the same eye color, brown, because the dominant allele is present in both.

But, bb, without a dominant allele to overtake the recessive form, results in blue eyes. You can see here that people with the same phenotype, such as brown eyes, can still have different genotypes behind them.

Thus, if my mother had the genotype BB and my dad had the genotype Bb, I would have brown eyes because my mother could only pass the B allele so it would not matter which one my dad passed to me. Because I have blue eyes, I know my genotype is bb because that is the only genotype that produces blue eyes.

This means each parent had to have a recessive b to pass along. Since they have brown eyes, I know they each must also have a B allele. Thus, we know with certainty, even without checking their DNA, that their genotype for eye color is Bb.

In a large population, there will be a pretty standard representation of these genotypes. About 25% will have BB, about 50% will have Bb, and about 25% will have bb. But, if you pick a very small number of individuals from a population, such as ten people, you likely will not find that exact percentage for each genotype represented in that small group.

For example, when we look at the population as a whole, we find that around 50% of people are male (genotype XY) and around 50% are female (genotype XX). OK, it's not exactly 50% in reality, but let us pretend it is for simplicity since I am demonstrating a point.

If we picked three families from the population with four children each, so 12 children total, it is unlikely that exactly six of those children would be boys and six girls.

But, if we randomly picked 200 families with four children each from the population, we would likely find that roughly 400 of the children were girls and 400 children were boys. Small groups do not often represent genotypes in equal proportions compared to the larger population. Keep this in mind as we move on to this next section.

PUNCTUATED EQUILIBRIA

Let us return to the example of the members of a population moving to a new island. In some cases, that movement is due to a passage opening for a period of time. In such cases, quite a few members of a population may make their way over to the new island before the passageway closes once again.

In this case, when many individuals migrate, the newly formed population will start out genetically similar to the original population from whence it came, changing only in response to the different selection pressures of the new environment. Change will happen slowly over the generations.

But, that is not how it always happens. A few migrant individuals may make their way over to a new island by floating on a piece of log or perhaps a couple of insects end up getting caught in a gust of wind that spurs or even necessitates their movement to the new island.

However these tiny populations get there, the point is when a very small number of individuals migrate from their original population, it is unlikely that they fully represent the gene pool that is present in the population they left.

For example, imagine 200 individuals move to a new island. The group likely has a similar genetic make up as a whole compared to the original population that they left. But, now, imagine two organisms, male and female, migrate alone to a new island. Both of them carry the genotype Aa.

In this case, 100% of the new population contains the genotype Aa rather than only 50%. The new population, therefore, is already genetically different than the population they broke away from. Suppose those two individuals create only two offspring, and, through chance, both of those offspring have the AA genotype.

Boom, the a allele for that trait is wiped out in a single generation. If the a allele led to a phenotype that was not advantageous and had been passed on in a large population, it would have slowly faded out over time due to natural selection. On the other hand, if the a allele led to a phenotype that was advantageous, it would have slowly increased over time.

However, whether it is advantageous or not does not matter in this scenario because random chance wiped it out. Consider that this situation can happen for many genes in that small population rather than just one. We can see how the members of the new population can change quite rapidly when compared to their original population.

Through this means, the process of evolution, or genetic change, can occur quickly as different selection pressures on the new island are acting on an already altered gene pool.

Thus, evolution can sometimes have more rapid bursts of change compared to other times.

This change does not only happen with migration, though. There are even more circumstances under which the genetic make up of a species or a population can change.

In the face of a sudden environmental change, many members of a population may be wiped out in a single generation, leaving behind only a small number of surviving individuals. In this case again, the small number of individuals likely does not represent the gene pool that once existed when the population was much larger.

Further, the environmental change often will create new, different selective pressures. So, once again, we see different selective pressures acting on an altered gene pool, escalating the rate of change within the surviving population.

The fossil record shows that the earth has undergone multiple events of mass extinctions due to large scale, catastrophic events and the resulting environmental changes. These periods of mass extinction are then followed by bursts of relatively rapid speciation (the formation of new and distinct species).

We have already considered how small, gradual changes over the course of a few billion years can easily lead to a wide variety of species from simple to complex. Now, we can see that with rapid bursts of evolution, it is all the more possible for us to start out with a bacteria and eventually, get a human being.

That said, there is not necessarily full agreement about the details of more rapid speciation and evolution amongst evolutionary biologists. There is still much left to be discovered. What we do know is that these events happen and when they do, we will see genetic change.

There is so much more to learn about evolutionary theory than this. If you have enjoyed learning this information and desire to learn more, I have provided suggested resources in the Additional Reading section.

I invite and encourage everyone to read and learn about our world. The earth tells a magnificent story, and it is worth the effort to hear it.

TESTING EVOLUTION IN A LAB

Remember the example I gave in which some lizards were released on a neighboring island and their change in traits over time was observed? The generation turnover for those lizards is two years.

That is pretty handy, but imagine how much more change we could observe if we could study an organism with a generation turnover measured in just hours. In fact, we can and have observed exactly that through a large number of carefully controlled experiments conducted in a lab.

The added beauty of these experiments is that we were able to observe literally tens of thousands of generations without ever once risking inadvertently causing an ecological catastrophe on an island, mainland, or body of water. We had everything to gain and nothing to lose.

These experiments have been carried out using bacteria. Bacteria have a very fast generation turnover rate. They are also affordable and relatively simple to house and care for when compared to many other species we could study.

One may wonder how we could study the evolution of bacteria and extrapolate those findings to much more complex beings like ourselves. The reason we can do so is that the same principles of natural selection that apply to bacteria apply to more complex organisms. While the organisms may differ in their complexity, the mechanism of natural selection is the same (review the section in this appendix, "More about DNA"). It does not vary between organisms.

Whether we are studying bacteria, fruit flies, sloths, or human beings, all living organisms have DNA composed of the same four building blocks that ultimately translates into the traits (phenotypes) those organisms have. Natural selection then acts on those phenotypes, and the genes that code for them, in the same manner for every organism.

Granted, reproduction happens differently. Bacteria reproduce asexually by essentially producing a copy of their selves. Sexually producing organisms reproduce by combining their genetic material with the genetic material of another member of their species. The resulting offspring then have a mixture of traits from two individuals rather than being a direct copy of just one parent organism.

Still, the principles of evolution occur the same way through random mutations within a gene resulting in traits that are either selected for or not selected for by the environment in which the individuals live. This process just happens much faster for bacteria because the generation turnover rate for bacteria is so rapid. And that is good news for us.

A bacteriologist named Richard Lenski, with the help of colleagues and his team, have studied evolution using bacteria for over thirty years. He began in 1988 by placing the species *Escherichia coli* (*E. Coliinto*) into each of twelve flasks along with a food source rich in glucose, creating twelve lines of bacteria that would never be mixed with one another.

Every day, a sample of bacteria is taken from each of the

twelve flasks and placed into a new one. This has been done every single day since the study began. In 2010, the team announced that they had observed 50,000 generations in the lab. If we were to observe this many generations of human beings, it would take well over one million years.

Occasionally, the scientists would collect bacteria from each of the flasks and freeze them, a way of creating their own little fossil record to which they could compare future generations and observe how they had changed.

As I mentioned, the bacteria were given glucose as their primary food source. Each day, the bacteria would initially explode in its rate of reproduction until the glucose was consumed. At that point, population growth would plateau as it was beginning to starve. A sample was then placed in a new flask with a new supply of glucose, and the process would begin again.

Glucose, therefore, was the limiting factor in the growth of the bacteria. One could hypothesize that the selective pressures would be for glucose utilization. Those that most efficiently utilize glucose would be expected to reproduce at a higher rate than those that do not utilize glucose as efficiently.

As generations would pass, one would expect that the colonies would become more and more efficient at utilizing glucose as a source of energy. And that is exactly what happened in all twelve lines of bacteria.

Samples taken from each line and then, compared to one of their fossilized ancestors showed that the bacteria became better at utilizing glucose over the generations. Interestingly, however, the different lines of bacteria did not necessarily achieve this at the same rate.

Some took a little longer to become more efficient than other lines. But, they all made it there. The researchers then sampled two lines to compare their DNA to one another and to their fossilized ancestors. Remember, these lines had never been mixed.

They found that both lines showed changes in 59 genes, and all 59 genes had changed in the same direction. The statistical odds of this happening by coincidence are astronomical. The probability of this happening by chance is so low, we may as well say the probability is zero. It happened through natural selection.

What this means is that in that environment, a specific genetic code is the most advantageous. As genetic mutations happen, those mutations that result in one of those 59 genes changing in a specific direction will be selected for, naturally. Those particular genes show up more and more until nearly everyone has all 59 of them.

So much data has been collected from this experiment with so many amazing discoveries and confirmations of aspects of evolutionary theory, one could write multiple books on the experiments conducted in this lab alone. What I have provided here is only one small piece of information we gained from these experiments. There are many more.

What we have observed in the natural world, we are testing in a controlled laboratory setting through these experiments and through many others. This experiment I described is only one of many. Evolutionary theory has undergone rigorous testing and, so far, it has consistently held up to the test.

If you would like to learn more about Richard Lenski's experiments, visit http://myxo.css.msu.edu/ecoli/

MORE ABOUT FOSSILS

The creation story of Genesis claims that the first life on earth consisted of seed-bearing plants and trees, which were created on day three. Interestingly, it also claims that the sun and moon were not created until the following day on day four (three days after light, day, and night were created, but I digress). In the story, God created light on the first day of creation, but he created the actual sun and moon on the fourth day, the day after creating plants. The creationists have multiple problems they must sort through here.

If they subscribe to young earth creationism, they believe the earth is less than 10,000 years old and that the earth and all life on it was created in a time frame of seven days. They have to explain why we have rocks that are over 3 billion years old. They have to explain why there are trees that are over 13,000 years old. They need to explain a lot.

As mentioned earlier in this book, some creationists subscribe to old earth creationism, meaning they believe that each of the seven days of creation was actually an era, perhaps thousands or even millions of years each. If this were true, that would mean plants managed to survive for thousands or millions of years without the sun as the sun was not created until the following era. Whether young earth creationist or old earth creationist, they all have a lot of detailed explaining to do.

The reality is that the oldest fossils we have found thus far are microscopic fossilized remains of *cyanobacteria*. They are 3.5 billion years old. The first life on earth did not consist of seed-bearing plants and trees. Did God skip these steps as he revealed the creation story to mankind?

Think of the unfathomable suffering that could have been avoided if God had simply let humans know of the presence of these microscopic organisms from the start. Germ theory would have been understood much sooner, and our ability to treat the illnesses caused by germs would have advanced much more easily.

It is no coincidence that the information God supposedly shared with mankind in the Bible shows a complete absence of any and all information mankind had yet to discover about the world at the time the Bible was written. If God wanted to show himself in this way, why not share information no human back then could have possibly known?

Why not share about the existence of bacteria? Then, when bacteria was ultimately discovered, scientists would see that the discovery fit perfectly with the information in the Bible. Why not reveal information about the fossil record that would eventually be found and studied?

Everything that we find in the fossil record contradicts the creation story in Genesis. Fortunately, the story the fossil record reveals is so much more grand and wondrous than the account we find in the Bible.

For most of the earth's history, for a few billion years, the only life on earth consisted of microbes and single-celled organisms. Multicellular organisms appeared only 600 million years ago. If God were indeed creating this world just for us, imagine the extreme patience this process would require (and we do not see such patience from the God of the Bible who seems to routinely fly off the handle over trivial occurrences).

From there, invertebrates came along and then, finally, our category, the vertebrates. All of this occurred in the sea. We have long worked to figure out how life moved from the sea to land.

Many different species and fossils have been studied in this endeavor. It is important to understand, though, that the discovery of a species that is very old does not necessarily mean that we have discovered one of our ancestral species from whom we descended.

For example, there is a species of fish that had lungs and lobed fins that moved in a step-like manner rather than producing swimming motions. These fish could breathe air and move around on land.

One could easily surmise that these creatures were the ancestors of those species who first crawled out of the sea and lived on land. Yet, they weren't. We know this because of the vast numbers of fossils we have. These creatures existed, and some still exist, but they were not in the particular line that led to the first land animals.

These organisms do not contain traits that we see in the organisms that lived on land. They do not have traits that are homologous with, or similar to, land animals. Remember that an organism's traits exist because it benefits that partic-ular organism at that particular time in that particular envi-ronment.

These fish with lungs and lobed fins did not have them for the purpose of providing a transition from sea to land. They had those traits because those traits served the organism well at that time. Thus, we cannot find such a crea-ture and instantly declare that this must be an ancestor to the species who lived on land. There are multiple paths through which life could have moved from the sea to land.

To determine the individual organisms on this specific path from sea to land, we must look for homologous traits. This means we look for similarities between different species and their various traits.

Fossilized specimens of other organisms have been discovered with fins that contain bones homologous with the humerus (upper arm bones) and radius and ulna (lower arm bones) in tetrapods. We also find smaller bones homologous with wrists and fingers. In another fin on these creatures, you find bones homologous with the thigh bone, shinbones, ankle bones, and foot bones of tetrapods (land-living vertebrates).

This information allows us to determine that the fish with lungs and lobed fins were not the ancestors to tetrapods. The lack of homologous traits reveals their line went in a direction, if it went anywhere at all. Evolution did not occur through one straight line in which all older species are the ancestors to all newer species. It is a branching tree going in many directions.

Meanwhile, looking at homologous traits, we can determine which fish were the ancestors of tetrapods. The fish that were ancestors to tetrapods had the beginnings of arms and legs in the skeletal structure within their fins. We find similarities in the spine and skull between these fish and the earliest tetrapods as well.

From there, we have fossils of fish that were even more tetrapod-like and so forth, tracing the lineage. Even though we do not have absolutely every single step filled in, enough steps are filled in to clearly reveal the history of life as it left the sea and established on land.

Creationists who attempt to attack the fossil record often show a gross misunderstanding of the concept I have just described. They point to the fish with lungs and lobed fins, describe how there are no similarities between them and the species who live on land, and then, declare that land animals could not have possibly descended from these fish.

Well, they are right. Tetrapods did not descend from those particular fish. But, that does not mean they are not products of evolution. They evolved from a different species entirely. Creationists decry that there are no transitional fossils between such species and therefore, evolutionary theory is incorrect. But, we do not have fossils between these species because neither of these species is ancestral to the other.

The only way to make creationism work in this way is to believe that evolution occurs in a direct, straight line. As already mentioned, the fossil record shows clearly that this is not how evolution occurred. Older species are not all parents of all other younger species just as elderly human beings are not all grandparents of all human children.

We see this from creationists most notably in the study of the recent evolutionary history of our own species and the many other human-like species that once lived on this earth. A large number of human-like species have existed on this planet, but they were not all our ancestors.

The visual often used to represent the evolution of man is a picture of a chimpanzee followed by a less chimp-like individual, followed by another even less chimp-like individual and so forth until we see a human being walking at the front of the line. Such an image is not complete, however.

This visual does not provide us with all of the branches alongside us that also contained human-like species from whom we are not descendants. The evolution of humans and human-like species is not a straight line. Creationists have failed to understand this. So, any time a discovery is made in which an extinct human-like species is learned to not be one of our direct ancestors, the creationists latch onto that discovery and declare that we are not products of evolution.

For example, neanderthals were very similar to our species. They had large brains, and they had a complex culture. They buried their dead and decorated the gravesites. There is evidence that they might have even believed in an afterlife, though we are not sure. They made and used axes, arrowheads, and other tools from bone and wood.

Neanderthal DNA can be found in modern humans. Upon considering all of this information, one could conclude that the neanderthal species must be ancestral to our own species and that we are direct descendants of that species. However, we did not evolve from neanderthals. They are actually not one of our ancestral species.

Neanderthals appeared after *Homo sapiens*. We could not have evolved from this species because we were here first. Neanderthals descended from a different line. They were more like cousins to our species, not parents.

The reason we find neanderthal DNA within our own is due to the fact that our genetic similarities allowed some interbreeding to successfully take place. Some individual neanderthals indeed are our ancestors, but the species as a whole is not an ancestor to our species as a whole.

When this information was announced, many creationists immediately claimed that evolutionary biology had just disproven evolutionary theory in entirety. But, none of this means we are not products of evolution. It simply means that we are not direct descendants of that particular species.

There are many human-like species that existed. We have found thousands of fossils of these various species. We still have much to learn, and we have not yet determined where they all fit in our lineage or whether each of them is a part of our lineage at all.

Still, we have a large number of high-quality specimens,

and we have gleaned a great deal of detailed information from them. In time, we will plug these species into the correct place on the evolutionary tree. In the meantime, the discovery that a species is one of our cousins rather than one of our grandparent species does nothing to disprove our evolutionary roots.

The fossil record is large and vast. To deny this truth is to be blind. The fossil record does not have to provide every single individual step from the spark of life to the diversity of life on earth today in order for us to see the obvious connections that exist within this record.

Everything about the fossil record supports the theory of evolution. New discoveries of fossils have only increased our knowledge of evolutionary history, they have never once disproven evolutionary theory in any way. The fossil record is rich, vast, amazing, and fascinating. If you would like to learn more about what we know from the fossil record, I strongly recommend reading Donald R. Prothero's <u>Evolution: What the Fossils Say and Why it Matters</u>.

ADDITIONAL READING

If you would like to learn more about the subjects I have touched on in this book, I have compiled a list of recommended reading (listed in no particular order).

- Climbing Mount Improbable by Richard Dawkins
- God is not Great by Christopher Hitchens
- Pale, Blue Dot by Carl Sagan
- Evolution: What the Fossils Say and Why it Matters by Donald R. Prothero
- The God Delusion by Richard Dawkins
- The Not-So-Intelligent Designer: Why Evolution Explains the Human Body and Intelligent Design Does Not by Abby Hafer
- Outgrowing God by Richard Dawkins
- The Man who Mistook his Wife for a Hat by Oliver Sacks
- Phantoms in the Brain: Probing the Mysteries of the Human Mind by V.S. Ramachandran and Sandra Blakeslee

- <u>Understanding Evolution</u> by E. Peter Volpe and Peter A. Rosenbaum
- <u>Baboon Metaphysics: The Evolution of a Social Mind</u> by Dorothy L. Cheney and Robert M. Seyfarth
- <u>Biological Psychology</u> by James W. Kalat
- <u>The Song of the Dodo</u> by David Quammen
- <u>The Hunt for the Dawn Monkey: Unearthing the Origins of Monkeys, Apes, and Humans</u> by Christopher Beard

If you are currently in ministry, have stopped believing, and do not know where to turn, visit The Clergy Project at <u>http://clergyproject.org</u>. For everyone else, please consider supporting this important organization.

Printed in Great Britain
by Amazon

35497807R00147